CHOOSE PANAMA...

...the PERFECT RETIREMENT HAVEN

WILLIAM HUTCHINGS

authorHOUSE

1663 Liberty Drive, Suite 200
Bloomington, Indiana 47403
(800) 839-8640
www.authorhouse.com

First published by AuthorHouse 08/05/04

ISBN: 1-4184-7804-0 (e)
ISBN: 1-4184-7803-2 (sc)

Library of Congress Control Number: 2004095317

Printed in the United States of America
Bloomington, Indiana

This book is printed on acid-free paper.

Choose Panama . . .

For Allison and Tony

To my daughters, Kimberly, Allison, and Kerry. With gratitude to fellow writer, Sandy Giedeman, and my fly-fishing pals, Ray Larson, Jim Congleton, and Dave Anderson for urging me to complete this book.

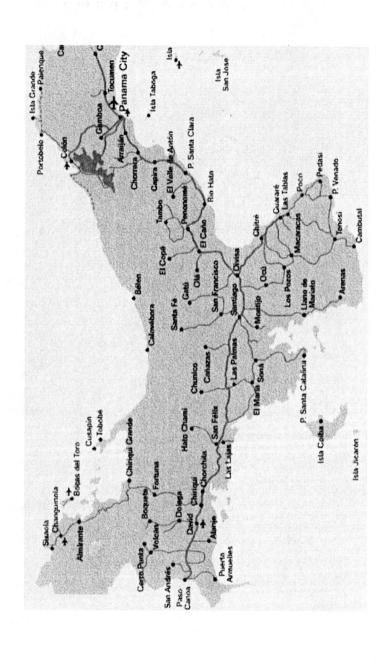

Table of Contents

William Hutchings

Choose Panama . . .

the Perfect Retirement Haven

by

William Hutchings

When I started the research on my new book,
friends would say, "Panama?   You're nuts.   Panama's
a jungle filled with crocodiles, snakes, and guerillas.
The mosquitoes look like flying grizzly bears."

8

With those few words of encouragement, I packed up a few things, my trusty laptop, my digital camera, and called American Airlines. I left the pith helmet at home.

Two and a half hours out of Miami, I woke from a nice nap and was greeted by darkening skies punctuated with snowy white cumulus clouds. As the plane banked for its final approach to Tocumen International Airport, I saw a crystal blue bay bordered with miles of glistening skyscrapers. For a moment, I thought we'd returned to Miami, but the Flight Attendant announced, "Panama City." Wow!

Hutchings   Panama Skyline   Bay of Panama

This book was written as a result of the author's quest for a retirement base. It had to be a place where the cost of housing and the overall cost of living could be accommodated on a fixed retirement income. Now, the Gobi desert might meet those financial considerations, but there are a host of other things to consider.

Panama was one of several potential choices. Its benefits and detractions were weighed against those of several countries: Mexico, Costa Rica, Nicaragua, Belize, Ecuador, and Argentina. Indeed, all of those countries have charm and advantages.

For the author's needs, Panama rose to the top. However, each reader thinking of a second home or of becoming an expatriate retiree, should do their own research on the countries they are considering.

Then weigh their assets and liabilities against those of Panama.

Choose **Panama. . . .** is <u>not</u> intended to be the ultimate Guide Book for vacationers. It is intended to be a reference manual to help you choose a retirement location or a second home. We assume that if you're serious about considering Panama as a choice for retirement or a second home, then you will visit before making your decision. To that end, we include many hotels, restaurants, and areas of interest as a convenience while you're looking the country over.

Examples of restaurants, places to stay, and other points of interest are listed here to meet a wide choice of budgets when you visit. The list is by no means complete, but it will give you some idea about the country, its accommodations, attractions, and prices.

Enough details on Panama are provided that will enable you to make a quality comparison with the other places you might be researching. Our main focus will be on the elements of day-to-day living costs, real estate, medical care, and the economic as well as political stability of the Republic of Panama. Perhaps most important, are the steps and paperwork you'll need to become a permanent resident with a Pensionado or other visa. We've provided the descriptions of these visas and how you can qualify.

Why *Choose* Panama?

Each of us, if we're lucky, will one day retire. Those with only Social Security, Military, or other government benefits are going to be hard-pressed to survive and maintain a reasonable standard of living – unless we can find a place whose cost of living will not exceed our retirement benefits. And, where the days ahead can be exciting and fulfilling – perhaps in an exotic setting.

Those with pensions, savings accounts, and home equity will want to be able to preserve their savings and still live comfortably in a community of their peers.

HOW WOULD YOU LIKE TO RETIRE?

- Where you can live comfortably on $1,200 a month?

- Where quality medical care and insurance is available?

- Where medical & dental costs are a fraction of U.S. costs?

- Where the paper currency is the U.S. dollar?

- Where you don't have to worry about currency devaluations?

- Where you can earn up to $76,000/year tax-free from Uncle Sam?

- Where there are a variety of climates – from temperate to tropical?

- Where you can choose beachfront, the mountains, or the city?

- Where you can buy an oceanfront lot for less than $40,000?

- Where you can rent a nice small home for $350/month?

- Where you can grow your own coffee?

- Where you can grow your own oranges, bananas, and vegetables?

- Where you can hire a maid for $6/day?

- Where infrastructure is First World?

- Where you can safely drink the water from the tap?

- Where the streets and roads are in good condition?

- Where you can fly back to the states in 2-1/2 or 3 hours?

- Where the government grants $$ incentives to foreign retirees?

- Where there's a variety of recreation – golf, tennis, birding?

- Where you can invest in certain businesses tax-free?

- Where Internet connections are readily available?

- Where satellite TV brings in your favorite programs – in English?

<u>Sound good?</u> . . . then consider <u>Panama!</u>

Panama has been the best-kept secret for retirement and as a tax haven in the Western Hemisphere - perhaps the world.

Modern Maturity, the monthly magazine published by AARP, listed **Boquete, Panama** as one of the four best places in the world to retire!

Perhaps you're already retired, or thinking about your upcoming retirement. There's always a little worry, a little voice that keeps asking, "Will I have enough retirement income to survive comfortably without eroding my savings and equity?"

". . . And, will my medical insurance cover any costs associated with a possible devastating illness? Will I like the culture? What's the climate like?"

To be practical, we must be able to answer those questions.

Perhaps you want to find a place where you can buy a home, use it for vacations, and rent it out the balance of the year until you finally do retire. This is certainly an option. If this is part of your plan, your rental income is tax-free of Panamanian income taxes.

To be sure, the world's finest retirement haven will not be a secret much longer. When considering the benefits and advantages that Panama offers, that 'secret' will become common knowledge - sooner rather than later.

And then you know what will happen? The same thing that happened in, California, Arizona, Florida and other "retirement communities." Prices will rise.

It is a fact that millions of "baby boomers" are fast approaching the age of retirement. Over 70 million within the coming decade. And, there are enough 'younger' retirees who can see their savings dwindle every month and should be considering an alternate home.

According to <u>Time</u> magazine, "Many of the 76 million American baby boomers are more likely than their parents to consider retiring to a foreign land because they have traveled more, have higher hopes for retirement, and tend to be more active and adventuresome."

It is a fact certain that many retiree's Social Security or other retirement benefits will not stretch to afford a comfortable standard of living in the U.S.

Each of us must ask the question, what kind of retirement can be anticipated where I currently live? With taxes, prices, medical care, insurance costs, and real estate escalating not only in the Western Hemisphere, but in Europe as well, it's going to be difficult to survive without some form of additional income.

As retirees, do we want to take part-time work at McDonalds or Wal-Mart to supplement our benefits? Not if we can retire to a paradise where a comfortable lifestyle is within the means of our benefits.

Of course there are a myriad of other questions besides the economics of Social Security or other retirement plans that must be answered.

Retirement Questions

- Is good medical care and insurance available?
- What's the cost of living?
- How about transportation?
- Is the climate desirable?
- How about housing?
- What will housing cost?
- Is the housing modern with modern conveniences?
- Is there a community of fellow expatriates?
- What about economic stability?
- What if I don't speak the language?
- Isn't Panama 'buggy' and miserably hot?
- How about safety, guerillas, and bandits?

Whether searching for a retirement haven, or seeking a place to vacation, Panama offers:

Near-perfect weather in a variety of locations.

A low cost of living.

A stable political and economic climate.

It's easily accessible: 2-1/2 to 4 hours from Miami, New Orleans or Houston. Six hours from Los Angeles, and the cost of the airfare is readily affordable. Language can be a problem, but it can be easily handled.

The Republic of Panama welcomes retirees with financial incentives not found anywhere in the world.

Two major factors have contributed to Panama's becoming such a major bargain for investment and real estate.

- On December 31, 1999, the United States turned over the complete operations of the Panama Canal to the Government of Panama, and abrogated the lease held on Panamanian property since 1904. Over 50,000 Americans left the country. This left a huge hole in the Panamanian economy. It is estimated the lost payroll was more than $400 million. That's a major cash deficit to overcome, especially when the country's entire revenue was only $2.4 billion.

- Panama is a major producer of fine coffee. World coffee prices have decreased more than fifty percent from the 1999 prices.

18

The reason for this massive price deflation is the introduction of cheap Asian beans, which have flooded the market. According to one report, there is so much excess coffee in Asia, the beans are being ground up for fertilizer. The deterioration of this market is having an economic impact on not only Panama, but all Central and South American countries who are primary coffee producers.

Of course, the 50,000 Americans who were called back to the United States also left a big hole in the real estate market. Especially, in Panama City. Houses, condominiums, and apartments are now selling and renting for bargain prices. The current opportunities for an investor or retiree are not better anywhere in the world.

Panama offers the retiree or investor a combination of economic advantages not available in other countries. Add these economic opportunities to a fine choice of climates, a country of near-zero inflation, a low cost of living, a stable political environment, and a country whose banking and asset protection laws offer privacy not even seen in Switzerland. And, there's a community of fellow expatriates in every city.

Put these factors together, and they all spell 'Panama'

Panama's Infrastructure

Panama City has a First World infrastructure (you can drink the water from the tap). The telephone system works reliably. Fiber-optic cables have been laid around the country and to Panama from overseas, enhancing telephone and internet connectivity. Air travel is reliable and frequent, within the country and overseas. Satellite TV is available throughout the country – from the U.S.

The Republic of Panama offers a Pensionado Visa program that grants unparalleled discounts on travel, restaurants, medical care, utilities, and entertainment to retiree expatriates. And to top it off, affordable, first-class housing is available.

Enjoy Panama's white sandy beaches, cool mountain slopes that burgeon with flowers, and the rich fragrance from hillside coffee plantations.

Enjoy its roads – better than any country's in Central America,

Enjoy its rain forests, and raft or fly-fish (for trout) the roaring rivers in the mountains.

Fish Panama's waters for the finest sport fishing in the world. More deep sea world records have been established in Panamanian waters than anywhere in the world.

Play golf or tennis at a world-class country club or convenient resort.

Enjoy the wonderful restaurants, luxurious hotels, and the safe environment.

Pinkerton's Global Security has recently named Panama as one of the four safest places in the modern world.

It's difficult to transcribe these advantages without sounding like they were penned by a tourist agency. In truth, the author was a skeptic about Panama and was nearly convinced to retire in Mexico, Puerto Rico, or Costa Rica. Then I visited Panama, and found it to be wonderful.

Panama is beautiful. Its people are beautiful. They're warm, friendly, and hard working. "Welcome" is written on their faces and reflected in their demeanor. Panama and the United States have been partners for many years, and Norte Americanos are welcomed.

Currency

Enjoy the security of a country whose paper currency is the U.S. dollar.

Think of it: there are no concerns about currency devaluations as you might have in other Central or

South American countries. And, there's virtually no inflation. Panama is the exception to the high rate of inflation predominant in so many countries south of the U.S. border.

Panama has put its act together, but until now, has not benefited from the tourist or retirement attractions it deserves. Remember the stories we've all heard from Florida, Arizona, and California, 'You should have been here ten years ago?' That's where Panama is today.

Recent statistics released from the World Tourism Organization show that the country's annual visitor count was slightly more than 400,000. More than 100,000 of these came from the United States.

Compare that figure with Disneyland: the amusement park's average daily attendance exceeds 160,000. In three days, Disneyland attracts more total visitors than Panama does in a year, and more visitors from the U.S. in a single day than Panama attracts from the U.S. in an entire year.

As a destination, Panama's tourism statistics aren't even close to the numbers of tourists or retirees visiting Mexico or Costa Rica. At least not yet. And what does that mean? It means those who get to Panama sooner rather than later will enjoy lower prices and can look forward to the value of their investments escalating.

Entry Requirements

Every visitor needs a valid passport and an 'onward' or return ticket.

Those visitors who are Naturalized citizens will need their Certificates of Naturalization.

A Tourist Card is required of everyone, and is sold for $5 by your airline prior to departure. Tourist Cards can also be obtained from Panamanian authorities after your arrival at Tocumen International Airport. They used to be valid for only 30 days, but are now valid for 90 days.

An **Exit Permit** is required of all visitors – no exceptions. The fee for a one-time departure is $20. A multiple entry/exit permit is available for $75. If you were to fly in and out of Panama several times, this is obviously more cost effective.

A word about traveling with minor children who accompany only one parent: a notarized letter of permission from the other parent is required.

The airlines will not issue a ticket without this letter. The purpose, of course, is to prevent one parent from leaving the country with children without authorization from the other parent.

For those countries whose airlines may have
overlooked this requirement, then immigration will
stop you from entering Panama.

Money

Panama's official currency is the *Balboa.* It is pegged
to the U.S. Dollar and has been since 1903. Coins for
Panama are minted in the U.S. Their size and value
are identical to our penny, nickel, dime, quarter, half
dollar, and silver dollar. There is NO Balboa paper
currency.

*All paper currency is the U.S. dollar. When you
come to Panama, do not bring denominations larger
than $20.*

If you're entering from a country other than the US,
**change your currency at the airport. Most banks
offer no currency exchange.**

Most stores simply will not accept $50 and $100 dollar
bills. Some of the larger hotels might, and the banks,
but they'll put the bills under a magnifying glass to
determine their authenticity.

But why go through the hassle? There are ATM
machines (called "Claves" - pronounced clah-vays)
everywhere, and most credit cards (Visa, Master Card,
and to a slightly lesser extent, American Express) are
widely accepted.

When using the Claves, always ask for a printed receipt. It is a bit disturbing, but your printed receipt will not show an account balance as they do in the U.S. You can reconcile the receipt when you actually check your balance. I used the internet phones ($0.20/minute for international calls) and called my bank's automated service every week or ten days to reconcile my ATM withdrawals.

Travelers Checks are also a hassle. Merchants – even hotels – don't like them. And personal checks? Forget it. Your ATM Card will become your best friend in Panama.

About Visas

- First of all, you need to be in Panama to obtain any visa. You cannot accomplish this in a Panamanian embassy or a consulate in your country. Most visas take three to four months to be issued (except for the Pensionado Visa, which is typically issued in three to four weeks).
- For most visas, an interim card is issued until the formal application is approved.

- You need to physically be in Panama <u>when the visa is issued.</u>

- It is also preferable that you stay in Panama from the time of the application until the issuance of the visa.

- The minimum age limit for a Pensionado visa is 18. <u>You don't have to be a senior citizen to qualify.</u> Children under 18 will qualify for their own visas as dependents of the parents.

- All documents from the applicant's country must be notarized and/or authenticated by the consulate office nearest you.

- For Canadian citizens, you should check with the Panamanian Embassy or the Consulate nearest your home.

Documents must be dated within two months of application.

- Spousal and juvenile dependents must have original marriage and birth certificates, respectively.

- Health certificates and AIDS certificates are required of all persons.

A visa is not a work permit. There are special rules for a work permit.

Permanent Visas

The Panamanian Government has developed a number of visa programs in order to attract investment in the country. Not only investors, but qualified immigrants who will help build Panama far beyond the developed state it enjoys today. And rest assured, the government's compulsory educational programs and dedicated philosophy to propel Panama into the future as a model country is similar to the philosophy instituted by the United States at the beginning of the twentieth century.

The programs outlined below are just that. Brief outlines. Not only must an attorney be employed to file your papers, you should consult a Panamanian attorney before ever investing, before the consideration of an investment, or thinking of a visa. Carefully go over the details of the outlines presented in this book, and then consult a Panamanian attorney to see which visa might be suitable for you.

Turista Pensionado Visa Program
(Visas for retirees)

Panamanian immigration laws authorize an alien to reside in Panama, provided they meet certain requirements. One of the most attractive residency programs anywhere is Panama's Pensionado program. It may well be the very best in the entire world.

A similar program was instituted in Costa Rica several years ago, and was very attractive. Thousands of expatriates immigrated to Costa Rica from all over the world. They signed up to be Pensionados, but the Costa Rican Government has retracted the program and none of the recipients were "grand fathered." They no longer enjoy the benefits that lured them to retire in Costa Rica.

Many of those people who went to Costa Rica have now immigrated to Panama where they not only benefit from the Pensionado program, but they now have a lower cost of living, a lower crime rate, and significantly lower real estate prices than in Costa Rica.

Panama's law specifically states that retirees who have qualified for the Pensionado program cannot lose their benefits. Period. So what are the qualification requirements?

- You must apply in Panama
- Your application must be processed by a Panamanian attorney
- You must be at least 18 years of age
- You must be of good health and free of HIV (A blood test costs $25 and a doctor's visit costs $10)
- You must have a verifiable minimum monthly income of $500 per month from a government program or private corporation. This could be Social Security or another

government retirement fund, such as military, state retirement, police pension, etc., or retirement from a private corporation.. For your spouse or minor children, your minimum income must be increased by $100 per month per dependent.

- You must have a certified, clear police record for the past five years. This can be obtained at your local police station or sheriff's office.
- All of the required documents must be notarized and authenticated at the Panamanian embassy or consulate office nearest your home. (see the glossary)
- If you don't have a retirement program, does that mean you can't get a Pensionado visa? Not at all. There are financial requirements that may be substituted:

  o A verified Certificate of Deposit in a Panamanian Bank that generates $750 per month for the retiree. The face value of the CD may vary because of interest rates offered by the National Bank of Panama. At the time of this writing, the approximate face value of the CD would be about $260,000. No additional amounts are required for dependents.

Pensionado Benefits

- A Pensionado Visa entitles the visa holder to a 50% discount on the price of admission to recreational and entertainment activities. Movies, sporting events, theatre events, concerts, etc. (Discounts do not apply where proceeds are designated for the benefit of charities.)

- Discounts on other services:

  - 50% on hotels, motels, and pensions Monday through Thursday, and 30% on Fridays, Saturdays, and Sundays
  - 50% discount on real estate closing costs and commissions for personal and commercial loan transactions in your name
  - 30 % on inter-urban and city buses
  - 30% on trains
  - 30% on charges for small boats and ships
  - 25% on air fares (Domestic)
  - 25% discount on your electrical bills if the monthly bill is less than $50
  - 25% discount on the fixed charge for personal telephone service (one telephone only)

o 25% discount on domestic water bills provided they don't exceed $10 per month
o 25% discount in restaurants (except for fondas – the small food servers not requiring a commercial license)
o 20% discount on general, specialized, or surgical fees
o 20% discount on technical and professional services
o 15% discount in fast food restaurants – those belonging to national or international franchises
o 15% discount on hospitalizations and medical clinics unless you have medical insurance
o 15% discount on dental services
o 15% discount on optometry services
o 10% discount on pharmaceuticals prescribed by a doctor
o 15% discount on interest rates charged by lenders on personal and commercial loans in your name
o <u>A freeze on personal residential real estate taxes</u> as long as the home is in your name
o Entitlement of a one-time exemption of duties on the importation of household goods (max of $10,000)

o   An exemption of duties every two
    years on the purchase of an
    automobile

The Pensionado Visa will <u>not</u> qualify a recipient
for a Panamanian passport or full citizenship, but it
will grant residency for life with the above benefits.
Most important, you do not have to leave the country
every 90 days as you do with a turista card.

Other Visa Programs

Rentista Retirado
(Private Income Retiree Visa)

For those retirees who are no longer working, but
have no monthly pension - perhaps having received a
lump retirement sum or inheritance.

This Visa requires money to be deposited in a five-
year Certificate of Deposit with the National Bank of
Panama. The amount to be deposited is to yield a
minimum of $750 per month (at current interest rates,
the face value of such a CD would be about $270,000.)
The Visa is renewable every five years as long as the
CD is renewed.

The Rentista Retirado Visa includes such benefits
as a Panamanian Passport, but does not include
citizenship. There is a one-year exemption of import
duties on household goods ($10,000) and the

exemption of duties for the importation of an automobile – every two years. The following requirements must be satisfied in addition to the monetary requirements above:

- Application must be made through a Panamanian attorney

- You must have a valid passport with at least one year before expiration

- Six passport sized photos – gentlemen in suit & ties, ladies in long sleeve blouses

- A police record from your place of residence, properly authenticated, for the past five years

- Marriage Certificate, notarized (if spouse is to be included)

Solvencia Economics Propia
(Person of Means Visa)

Designed for those persons who wish to live in Panama off their own means, without the need to work.

The person must make a one-year Certificate of Deposit in a local bank of at least $100,000. Upon application for the first renewal (provisional) the CD must also be renewed for one year.

After renewal, the visa is granted permanently with the right to a cedula (a local Identity Card). Five years after obtaining the permanent Visa, holders will be eligible to apply for Panamanian nationality.

The following requirements must be met to apply:

- Valid passport (with at least one year before expiration)

- Six passport photos (same as per Rentista Retirado)

- Police Record from your city of residence (Five years)

- Marriage Certificate (notarized) if your spouse is to be included

- Monetary requirements as above

Inversionista
(Investor Visa)

Designed for those who want to establish a business in Panama. Please note: all retail businesses and some professions are reserved for Panamanian citizens. Please check with your attorney.

There must be a minimum investment of $100,000 and at least three permanent Panamanian residents hired. This visa is granted provisionally for one year. After renewal, it is granted permanently, and a cedula (Panamanian I.D. card) can be issued. Five years after permanent status is granted, holders may apply for Panamanian citizenship.

The following requirements must be met upon application:

- Valid Passport with one year before expiration
- Six passport photos (as in above)
- Police record (authenticated) from your city of residence for past five years
- Marriage certificate (authenticated) if your spouse is to be included
- Monetary requirements as shown above

Inversionista de Pequena Empressa
(Small Business Investor Visa)

This visa is established for those people who wish to start a small business in Panama.

You must invest a minimum of $40,000 and hire three Panamanian permanent employees.

This visa is granted provisionally for one year. It must be renewed three times before it is granted permanently, whereupon a cedula may be issued. Five years after obtaining the permanent visa, holders will be eligible for Panamanian citizenship.

The following requirements are required for application:

- Valid passport with more than one year before expiration

- Six passport photos as in above requirements

- Police record, duly authenticated

- Marriage certificate (authenticated) if spouse is to be included

- The financial requirements listed above

- This visa will also require setting up a Panamanian corporation and appropriate bank accounts.

Inversionista Forestal
(Forestry Investor)

Designed for those who want to make long-term investments in re-forestation projects.

There must be a minimum investment of $40,000 into an Accredited re-forestation company. This investment must be held until final harvest of the trees, about 15 years.

This visa is granted provisionally for one year. After the one year period it can be renewed and will then be granted permanently with the right to be issued a cedula. Five years after obtaining the permanent visa, holders will be eligible to apply for Panamanian citizenship.

The following requirements are necessary for application:

- Valid passport with more than one year before expiration

- Six passport photos as in above requirements

- Police record, duly authenticated

- Marriage certificate (authenticated) if spouse is to be included

- The financial requirements listed above

Forestry products, Teak in particular, offer long range profit potential. The bulk of the world's teak supplies have traditionally come from Myanmar (formerly Burma). The Myanmar's have consistently over-harvested their trees, and the National Geographic reports that the Myanmar teak forests will be logged off by 2010.

Panama has always maintained significant teak forests (in the Darien Region), and with a technologically and ecologically sound forestation program, Panama promises to be the world's leading exporter of teak products.

Investment in this program will grant you immediate residency rights, and after five years, you will be eligible for a Panamanian passport.

Further information is available at the Ministry of Agriculture, Panamanian Environmental Agency. Also, see the Business Opportunities section.

Not all retirees are satisfied to retire. They may want to remain active. Panama offers a unique opportunity to do both.

Business Opportunities

Panama enacted Law # 8 in 1994. This legislation enabled the promotion of tourism and foreign investment. And to date, it's the most comprehensive legislation to facilitate investment anywhere in Central or Latin America.

Many of the world's largest hotel chains, including, Marriott, Radisson, Holiday Inn, Sheraton – with more to come – have launched new hotels in Panama. And, there's more than $500 million in projects being planned on Panama's coming of age as a tourist destination.

But the legislation is not just for the giants of the industry. Anyone willing to invest as little as $50,000 in a tourist related business can take advantage of the law, which grants large tax and financial incentives.

Hutchings   Punta Paitilla

For instance, several people I know have bought property, built a home and a guest-house and they receive, (with a minimum investment of $50,000) the benefits outlined below. They rent the guest-house like a bed and breakfast, an apartment, or mini-hotel.

Others have started charter diving operations on Bocas del Toro, or a River Rafting business. Or, you might start a touring business for eco-tourists, bird watchers, etc.

The benefits are substantial for any tourist related business:

- A 20 year exemption of any import taxes due on materials, furniture, equipment, and vehicles
- A 20 year exemption on real estate taxes for all assets of the enterprise
- Exemption from any taxes levied for airports and piers
- Accelerated depreciation of real estate assets of 10% a year.

The investment of $50,000 does not include the cost of land, and the program is limited to projects in the interior, i.e., Boquete, Volcan, El Valle, etc. These specific regulations can change, so be sure to go over them carefully with your attorney.

For more information on Panama's investment incentives for tourism related businesses, go to the internet: www.ipat.gob.pa

Real Estate, Tourism, and Forestation projects are some of the more popular for individual investors.

Panama is one of the most technologically advanced countries in Central or South America. Communications are the backbone of any nation's future, and Panama has state of the art communications infrastructure with multiple high band-width fiber optics networks.

Of course, Panama's strategic location at the mid-point of the Americas has been, and will continue to be, a critical advantage for long-term development. As industry grows in Asia, transportation to the Eastern seaboard of the U.S. and Western Europe is most easily reached through the canal.

In real estate, there are properties available from the government that were part of the compounds originally built by the U.S. and then handed to the Republic of Panama with the abrogation of the Canal Treaty by Jimmy Carter and the U.S. Senate under his administration.

The port city of *Colon* is the second largest free port in the world, exceeded by only Hong Kong. Colon is on the Atlantic side of the Canal. Consequently, a huge amount of commerce, import and export, is being conducted. The opportunity to set up an import-export business in Panama is outstanding because of these facilities.

Real Estate

Many visitors coming to Panama are obviously interested in the real estate opportunities. They are excellent.

Words of Caution

- As stated earlier, it is important that you engage an attorney <u>before making an offer on any property.</u> This is true whether you have engaged a real estate agent or not. (This will not apply on property being developed and offered as new homes from developers such as Pan-Am Construction or Valle Escondido)

- Do not judge values based upon prices at home – whether you're from the Americas or Europe.

- Unfortunately, some 'gringo' real estate operators can be found who are guilty of the most blatant 'puffery' imaginable, e.g., "Buy now, because tomorrow it'll be double in price. There's very little left and the market is exploding!"

- They may make claims and statements comparing Panama with California, Aspen, Florida, etc.

- **<u>Insist on sales comparables</u>**

If the seller or person showing the property says, "They aren't available," then you'll have a pretty good idea the quoted price may be puffery. Comps are available, and your attorney can get reasonably accurate sales data from the National Registry, which records all real estate transactions. *Caveat Emptor!*

Casco Viejo – Renovations

Casco Viejo was built after Henry Morgan sacked and destroyed the original Panama City. It was burned by the Spaniards to keep Morgan from occupying the city. It's located on a small peninsula near the western entrance to the Panama Canal, and in all of the Americas, it's the oldest city on the Pacific Coast.

Marni   Casco Viejo Balconies

The buildings are French and Spanish Colonial in architecture. The streets are narrow and mostly cobblestone or brick. The grill-work on the balconies is fancy wrought iron.

The French moved in to build their canal, and built their colonial buildings in the late 19th century beside the original Spanish colonials. In places, there is a 300-year difference in the age of buildings sitting side by side.

As the city modernized and grew, the narrow brick and cobblestone streets were not adequate for the traffic, so the city expanded away from Casco Viejo.

In 1977, UNESCO classified Casco Viejo as a World Heritage site. At that time, the government realized what a treasure it had in the community and initiated a plan for restoration.

Most of the buildings were in some stage of dis-repair – even decay, but some structures have been fastidiously maintained. Many local families have stayed through the years in Casco Viejo. Many of these the nation's wealthiest.

Panamanian Law #9 was created to give incentives to property developers who renovate buildings in Casco Viejo. After renovation, all income derived from the sale or rental of the property is exempt from income taxes for a period of ten years. In addition,

100% of the cost of renovation is deductible from any other Panamanian Income tax you might owe.

Property taxes are exempt for a period of thirty years, and real estate transfer taxes are excused.

Hutchings   Casco Viejo Renovations

Parking in Casco Viejo is limited, so a parking garage is an excellent opportunity. Income is tax free for ten years.

Casco Viejo is a large area. It will take time to fully renovate, but progress is being made, and the results are spectacular. Be sure to visit Parque Bolivar to see an excellent example and architectural beauty of what can be done. Most of the buildings surrounding this beautiful small park have bee renovated.

Renovation from the Plaza de Independencia, up to the Presidential Palace and along Panama Bay to the French Embassy is going under a great deal of growth.

William Hutchings

Hutchings   Casco Viejo Apartments

If property development is in your area of investment expertise, don't miss the opportunity provided by the government in Casco Viejo.

Hutchings   Casco Viejo

Reforestation Investments

Much of the world's exotic hardwoods are grown in the tropics. Teak, Mahogany, Coco Bolo (Rosewood), and others are a few of the wonderful woods that are now in short supply. Teak in particular has been over-logged – especially in the far-east countries of Thailand and Myanmar (formerly Burma). Thailand's exports have been reduced to a trickle, and the National Geographic estimates that Myanmar will be out of production by 2010.

Panama has the soil, rainfall, humidity levels, and an ambient temperature conducive for teak production. In many instances, Panama's production and growth of their teak forests has reached optimum conditions not achieved anywhere in the world – including Myanmar. Not only is the re-forestation program doing well in the Darien, but other teak farming has started near David, in Chiriqui Province.

It is estimated that a $40,000 dollar investment in a three plus acre teak farm will return a reasonable multiple of that investment when the trees are ready for harvesting in 20 years. The investment is long term, but generally, a percentage of the investment can be recaptured from the three initial thinnings – between the sixth and eighth year. Of course, inflation and teak prices could increase significantly, yielding a multiple of these figures.

Teak forests are usually planted about 1,000 trees per hectare (2.47 acres). Initial cuttings (thinnings) may yield saleable wood. One local arborist estimates that by the eighth year, the yield from the first thru third thinnings might return some of the original investment. By the 8th year, the trees have been thinned enough for them to achieve optimum growth and to reach maturity without further thinning. Final count per hectare is about 700 trees. At maturity (20-25 years), a teak tree will yield approximately 400-500 board feet of wood. The current value of teak is about $2.00 per board foot.

For details regarding reforestation, go to: www.panamadera.com

A local study, near David, is being conducted jointly by Yale University, and the Smithsonian Institute.

Since a Teak reforestation project is a long-term investment, Panamadera is looking at an interesting concept: a four-hectare (almost 10 acres) section planted in half teak and half pineapples. Each of these sections will qualify under the government's reforestation guidelines for residency. This program is in the development stage and is not yet an actuality.

The area has rich, volcanic soil. The pineapples are expected to yield a 100% return on the investment in five years (at today's pineapple prices). They will continue to be harvested during the entire growing term of the teak plantation. Mr. Barker's U.S. associate is Mr. Randolph Hancock, (617) 901-3511.

Again, the author has no interest in any of the projects detailed in the Business Opportunities Section or elsewhere in this book. Their accuracy is unverified and must be pursued with diligence. They are presented here simply as potential opportunities for the investor or retiree.

Where to Retire – the City or the Country?

Now that we've outlined many of the benefits and many of the permanent visa opportunities, let's look at the country as a whole and give specifics on places you might like to consider.

For your convenience, while looking at several potential retirement locations, we'll list a few hotels, restaurants, and places to go, but certainly not all of them. There are other excellent Guide Books, such as Lonely Planet's, "Panama,"_that will give you detailed vacation information.

We want to give you a broad perspective of what Panama can offer you as a potential retiree, and details on visas that are available. At the same time, a few facts on the country in general are in order – especially about places to stay, restaurants, and the real estate and investment market.

Hutchings   Carmen Iglesia

Panama City

Hire an English-speaking guide if you don't speak
Spanish! The skyline of Panama City is spectacular.
Modern skyscrapers stretch upward, the sun reflecting
from their glass walls. Tall palm trees line the avenues
skirting the ocean.

Hutchings   Skyline: from Amador Causeway

It is definitely a cosmopolitan city and ranks with
Buenos Aires as the best in Central and South
America. No smog, noxious fumes, or poor air quality
to choke your breathing. Best of all, there is decidedly
less traffic congestion than in Miami, Mazatlan, and
Mexico City.

As you tour the city, there are other neighborhoods
to consider as residential options.

- Marbella is generally a community of high-rise
  apartments and condominiums, bordered by
  Balboa Avenue and Calle Cincuenta. It affords
  wonderful views of Panama Bay. This is also
  an area of night clubs, restaurants and chic
  shops. It adjoins the financial district.

- Punta Paitilla is an affluent area dominated by
  high-rise apartment and condominium
  buildings. The views are superb. Most
  residents are wealthy Panamanians or
  immigrants from other Latin American
  countries. There is a nearby waste disposal
  facility, so check any building in which you
  have an interest several times during a day for
  odor.

- El Congrejo is a hilly area of high rises and
  single family residences. It is centrally located
  near Via Espana and the University. It also

boasts of having many fine restaurants and apartment hotels.

- La Cresta is a very affluent community of older, lovely homes and buildings. Many expatriates live here as well as the U.S. and French Ambassadors. Most homes have beautiful Bay views.

- Obarrio is adjacent to the central banking district. Many fine residences are in this upscale neighborhood, and it is also the home of most of the up-scale retail shops in Panama City.

There are other areas of the city that are appropriate for expatriates. Have your guide or real estate agent direct you.

Shopping

Panama City is a shopper's paradise. Prices are very reasonable, whether you're looking for furniture, electronics, clothing, food, or souvenirs. Every imaginable product, from the latest in electronics to designer clothing, is readily available. Bargains are the rule. Colon is a major free port, second in world size only to Hong Kong.

For comparison, a new car in Panama is roughly half the price of the same car's price in Costa Rica. For this reason, Panama is not only a bargain when it comes to automobiles, but every other imported electronic and major appliance.

In addition to the stores and bazaars concentrated on Via España, shops are located on Avenida Central and several large malls throughout the city. Price Smart (Costco affiliates) stores are in Panama City as well as in the city of David – on the Pacific coast – in

Chiriqui province. PriceSmart honors the U.S. Costco membership card.

For some real bargains, take the train to Colon (about one hour on an elegant, interesting trip, and shop in the free port of Colon. The train does not return until 5:15 PM, but a taxi back is inexpensive. (Be watchful for pickpockets, and purse snatchers in Colon).

Villegas   Typical Shopping Mall

A U.S. quality supermarket chain, Supermercado Rey, is on Via España as well as in several other

53

locations. It's open twenty-four hours, 365 days per year. Supermercado Rey stocks everything from alcohol to pharmaceuticals. And, clothing is inexpensive. Don't pack heavily, because you can buy everything you need in Panama.

Bars, restaurants, and discotheques are everywhere. Panamanians love to dance. The Salsa, meringue, and reggae are popular, and everyone seems to perform them expertly. Great fun to watch. And, great fun to mix in and learn. Hotels run the gamut from five-star to pensións.

Villegas   Bucaneros Restaurant   Amador Causeway

Do We Have to Speak Spanish?

The simple answer is "no." English is a required subject in all Panamanian schools, and it's estimated that 25% of the population now speaks English. However, if you're going to live in Panama, you should make every effort to learn at least some

Spanish. The people will appreciate you all the more if you try to speak their language, even if you struggle and you're anything but fluent. People will help you and respect you for trying to learn.

Is Spanish difficult to learn?

If you're of retirement age, it's more difficult than if you were a child. But people do it every day. Consider studying Spanish as a project and make it fun. As a matter of fact, it's a great way to become acquainted with other expatriates.

Won't just being around the people day in and day out make it easy to learn?

Not a bit. Your chances of picking up conversable Spanish this way are close to zero. There are better ways:

- CD's that teach basic Spanish are available in most book stores. Also, if you have a computer, there are programs that are quite good. These cost between $20 and $35. Before you leave for Panama, get a head start. Buy one of these programs and practice.

- CentroPan USA (232-6718) offers a four week course, two hours/day, four days/week for $205 in Panama City. U.S.

Foreign Service personnel use this school.
It's very good,
but the intensity level of instruction is less
than in a 'total immersion' course.

- Hire a private tutor. The tutor will come to
your hotel room for $10/hour, or give six
lessons for $50. (One popular teacher is Sr.
Abdiel Marin, 507-268-1835)

- Berlitz is world-renowned for their
language courses. You could start one at
home, buy a Berlitz Home-study course, or
take their course in Panama City. Sra.
Leonora Lung de Smith is Directora in
Panama City, 507-265-4800, in Plaza
Balboa. She recommends studying the
Berlitz CD at home then taking their 3-hour
a day immersion course when you get to
Panama.

- Language & International Relations
Institute (LERI)
Tel: (260-4424) Four hours of daily
instruction, five days/week. Class is
limited to four students. The price of $350
for the first week includes lodging, two
meals/day, laundry, etc. Rates decrease
each succeeding week. They have a U.S.
Agent (Dana Garrison) 1-800-765-0025,
who is very helpful.   You can view the
website at: www.isls.com

This is 'immersion' learning. You lodge
with an upper-middle class family, and
continue to learn with them after your four
hours of schooling. This is an outstanding,
fast way to become conversant in Spanish.
And it's fun. They also teach you to Salsa
and take you out to clubs for even more
fun.

<u>Author's Note</u>: I had serious doubts about
immigrating to a country where I didn't speak a
little of the language, although I knew it wasn't an
absolute necessity. The author's aunt had retired to
a foreign country, lived there 10 years, and knew
little beyond 'yes,' 'no,' 'please,' and 'thank you.'

Even though a good percentage of
Panamanians speak some English, I was
uncomfortable not being able to speak their
language, so I decided to take the ILERI course. I
learned enough Spanish in a week to get along
quite well as I traveled throughout Panama. Every
day, I became more comfortable speaking with the
people. And every day as I stumbled along, I
received smiles, warmth, and lots of help.

The course was great. The instructors were
wonderful. The 'family' I stayed with was
friendly, hospitable, and the time spent with them
was terrific. The food was better than good. I
believe I can count my hosts as being my first new

friends in a new country, and I would not trade this experience for anything. Home-stay house below.

Social Customs – Do's & Don'ts

Panama is more formal than you might expect. This definitely applies to dress. Just because the country is in the tropics, sandals, torn jeans, and cut-off shorts are not acceptable attire in banks, business establishments, or government offices. (They're fine in Bocas del Toro)

In the evening, whether it's a restaurant, club, or disco, men and women "dress." For the men, the very least should be slacks and a shirt with collar. The loose fitting 'Guayaberra' shirt (available everywhere in Central America) seems to be universally accepted. Incidentally, when in the tropics, cotton is the fiber of choice. The synthetics don't 'breathe' as well They're 'hotter,' and not nearly as comfortable as cotton. When buying clothes, look on the label for – Algondon – it means cotton.

Drugs are not tolerated in Panama. If you are even in the proximity of someone using marijuana or cocaine, move away. Police might assume you have some connection if you're just nearby. And in Panama, you're considered guilty until proven innocent. Accusation of a serious crime (drugs are considered a serious crime) generally results in jail time. It can be months before a trial date is set, and your embassy cannot help you.

Always carry your passport, your tourist card, or a Xerox copy, or something with you at all times with a photo ID. It's the law.

Always say, "gracias" when thanking someone. Always say, "por favor" as please. The standard greeting is "Hola" for hello, "Buenos Dias" for Good Morning, and "Buenas Noches" for Good night. The Panamanians are very polite, and that politeness should be reciprocated.

Places to Stay – Panama City

There are many fine hotels in Panama City. There are also many hotels offering good accommodations at lesser prices. We will try to name a few in a broad range of price and amenities. One thing to bear in mind: Always ask for a commercial rate – whether you're on business or vacation. Many times the desk clerk will give you a lower price.

As for hotels in the $7-$15 range, they do exist. Especially, in the Casco Viejo district. For the purpose of this book, we will not do a hotel-by-hotel listing of these hotels, but there are several available. Most of the rooms at the lower prices are not air-conditioned, baths are generally shared, and most do not have hot water, but some of them fill a need and do it nicely.

One of the newer "residencia" establishments is the "Cibeles" on Calle Equador. An associate of mine stayed there for $15/night (single) and reported it to be very clean, comfortable, air-conditioned, and with private bath.

Mid-Range Hotels

* Prices shown are for 'single/double'

- Hotel Marparaiso – $20/$25   Tel:227-6767. Calle 34 Este between Avenidas 2 & 3. Built 1999, 72 large rooms, well-appointed. A/C, cable TV, telephones, secure parking.

- Hotel California - $21/$33 Tel: 263-7736 Avenida Central Espana near Calle 43.   58 nice clean rooms, color TV, phones, restaurant & coffee bar in lobby.

- Hotel Internacional - $22/$27 Tel:262-7806 Opened in '90's, so it's relatively new. Faces Plaza Cinco de Mayo. 80 rooms, A/C, cable TV, Restaurant & casino. (hint@latin1.net)

- Hotel Lisboa - $22/$24 – Tel: 227-5916   On Avenida Cuba between Calles 30 Este and 31 Este. Spacious, attractive rooms, A/C, TV & phones. Good value.

- Hotel Caribe - $27-$34 Tel: 225-0404 Calle 28 Este at Avenida Peru. Spacious, A/C Rooms, phone, cable TV, refrigerators, ice machines, pool on the roof. Another good value. (caribehotel@hotmail.com)

- Las Vegas Suites Hotel - $35/40 Tel: 269-0722 Calle 49B Oeste & Avenida 2A Norte. All rooms have kitchenettes, A/C, cable TV & phones. Café Pomodoro & The Wine Bar. Very popular. (hotel@lasvegaspanama.com)

- Gran Hotel Soloy - $39-$43 Tel: 227-1133 Avenida Peru at Calle 30 Este   Nice rooms, A/C, Cable TV. Casino on ground floor and bar & dance club on 12th floor. (hgsoloy@pan.gbm.net)

- Hotel Costa Inn - $44/$50 Tel: 227-1522 Avenida Peru near Calle 39 Este. 130 rooms, A/C, Satellite TV, Internet, Gym, Pool, good restaurant, secure parking, airport shuttle, & tours available. This hotel gets high marks. (costainn@panama.c-com.net)

Luxury Hotels

There are many 'luxury' hotels in Panama City. So many, we can't list them all. Prices shown are standard, 'walk-in off the street, rack rates.' One hotel where I stayed is listed at a rate of $100+. The author made a reservation over the internet for $60 during the height of the holiday season. (They were <u>not</u> informed I was a travel writer.)

- Hotel Costa del Sol (do not confuse with Hotel Costa Inn) $55-$60 Tel: 206-3333 Avenida 3 Sur at Avenida Federic Boyd. Each A/C room has a kitchenette.   Swimming pool, restaurant, and bar on the roof. Also, tennis court and Spa. Wonderful views. (<u>www.costadelsol-pma.com</u>)

- Coral Suites Aparthotel - $50+ Tel: 269-3898 Via Italia (Calle "D") & near Calle 49B   Very comfortable with gym, rooftop pool, laundry, internet connections, satellite TV, etc. Breakfast is included. Larger suites are available for families. The gym includes free weights, exer-cycles, treadmills, and weight machines. Pool and laundry facilities are outstanding.   This would be a $250 suite in metropolitan cities in the states. (***coralsuites@coralsuites.net***

Choose Panama . . .

Hutchings   Coral Suites, Roof-top Pool

- Crystal Suites Hotel - $65/$75. Tel: 263-2644 Avenida 2 Sur and Via Brasil. Newer hotel. Attractive executive suites with kitchen and dining area. Internet service, airport shuttle. Lovely hotel, a little isolated. (atencion@crystalsuites.com)

- Sevilla Suites - $65-$85 Tel: 213-0016 Avenida 2A Norte   This is an all suites hotel (opened in 2000). All suites have a sofa bed, cable TV, VCR's, & kitchenettes. Facilities include a roof-top pool, coin laundry, gym, breakfast included. This hotel is family owned and operated. It is a superior place to stay. Under the same ownership is the Hotel Marbella. It is modern, clean, and well appointed, but no suites. Price is $55. (sevillasuites@sevillasuites.com)

- Hotel Plaza Paitilla Inn - $80+   Tel: 269-1122
  Via Italia at Avenida Churchill. A former
  Holiday Inn. Hotel is on the water & all rooms
  have balconies. Lovely pool, and the hotel has
  a very popular bar.
  (www.plazapaitillainn.com)

- Panama Marriott Hotel $89+ Tel: 210-9100
  Avenida 3 Sur 296 Rooms, restaurant & bar,
  offers concierge, childcare, etc. Fine business
  hotel. Includes buffet desayuno (breakfast).
  (www.mariotthotels.com)

- Radisson Royal Panama Hotel - $99+ (Special
  discounts for seniors) Tel: 265-3636 Calle 53
  Este at Avenida 5B Sur. Elegant hotel, tasteful
  rooms, pool, coffee shop, restaurant, piano bar,
  tennis court, gym. (www.radisson.com)

- Holiday Inn (new) - $99+ Tel: 206-5556
  Avenida Manuel E Batista & Avenida 2A
  Norte. 112 deluxe rooms, 38 suites, all have
  many amenities. Restaurant, pool, gym,
  arcade, sports bar.
  (holidayinn@holidayinnpanama.com)

- Miramar Inter-Continental - $99+ $185   Tel:
  214-1000 Avenida Balboa near Avenida
  Federico Boyd 25 Story, 206 rooms.
  Gorgeous guest rooms, wonderful views.
  Informal seaside restaurant and a fine dining
  restaurant on 5th floor. Other features include a

piano lounge, a bar and dance club, pool, spa & gym, tennis courts etc. Celebrities are frequent guests. (www.interconti.com)

- Suites Ambassador – Under $100. Tel: 263-7274 Calle D near Eusebio A Morales Very large rooms w/sitting area & Kitchenette. Rooftop pool. 1st class service. (ambassad@sinfo.net)

- The Executive Hotel - $100/$110   Tel: 264-3333 Avenida 3 Sur & Calle Aquilino de la Guardia Modern hotel with large, well furnished rooms, a complimentary breakfast and nightly open bar for guests, (pool, restaurant, and business center. Popular hotel among business crowd. (hotelger@pty.com)

- Hotel El Panama - $105/$120 Tel: 269-5000 Calle 49 B Oeste near Via Espana. An older landmark, yet fine hotel, with spacious poolside rooms. Wonderful bar, music, etc. for the true flavor of Panama.

Hutchings   El Panama

Hotel Granada - $100/$130 Tel: 264-4900
Calle Eusubio A Morales near Via Espana. Fine,
comfortable hotel. Every room A/C. Pool,
casino, restaurant & bar. I stayed at this hotel.
Rooms clean, etc. but you might try the Coral
Suites or Sevilla Suites for a little more room.
(granada@hotelesriande.com)

- Hotel Caesar Park - $99 (lowest promotional
  rate) to $800. Posted rate is $145+ Tel: 270-
  0477; (U.S.) 800-228-3000 Across from
  Centro Atlapa on Calle 77 Este near Via Israel.
  Part of Westin chain. Frequented by celebrities
  and heads of state. Facilities include casino,
  sports bar, shops, athletic club & spa, 3 tennis
  courts, club, business center, and more. Dining
  is elegant and views magnificent from 15th
  floor dining room. (www.caesarpark.com)

- The Bristol $125+ Tel: 265-7844 Calle Aquilino de la Guardia near Calle 50. Part of the Rosewood Hotels & Resorts. Very elegant. Marble & mahogany everywhere. All guests are provided with a personal butler and printed business cards. Dining is superb. Service is extraordinary. Each room has fax machine and internet. Tour their website: www.thebristol.com ; ejventas@psi.net.pa

For each of these hotels, from the more modest to the elegant, ask for their commercial rate and any "specials" or promotions they might be having on your expected arrival date. You'll save some money.

If you qualified for, and received your Pensionado visa, prices can be reduced by as much as 50% during the week and 30% on the weekends!

Restaurants – Panama City

Just a few of the hundreds of restaurant choices are listed below. Rather than categorize these by price, we've listed them by the type of food served.

In addition to these, most of the fast-food restaurants are here: McDonalds, Burger King, KFC, Pizza Hut, etc.

In most restaurants the servers understand English. If you should find one where communication is difficult, just ask for help at an adjoining table. People are friendly and glad to help.

- **Panamanian Food**

  o ***Restaurante-Bar Tinajas*** Calle 51, Bella Vista, 22 (206-7890) Very large restaurant. Décor is Panamanian. Long menu. Dinner prices average $7.50-$9.50. Panamanian entertainment and folk dancing on Fridays & Saturdays. Closed Sundays.

  o ***Café de Asis*** – Faces Parque Bolivar in Casco Viejo. Charm isn't descriptive enough. A wonderfully restored colonial building. It's an atmosphere where Graham Greene, John Le Carre, and Ernest Hemingway might meet at the next table. Don't miss this one. People-watching is one of the best things at Café de Asis – even if it's not on the menu!

  o ***Café Coca Cola*** – near Parque Santa Ana. 7:30 AM to 11:30 PM. Very popular. No breakfast items more than $2.50. An extensive lunch & dinner menu of chicken, beef, and fish. Most under $4.50. Specialty: jumbo prawns @$6.00.

o *Restaurante Costa Azul* – Calle Ricardo Arias near Via Espana. Very popular, open 24 hours. Sandwiches $1.50-$4.00. Dinner (wide variety of pasta, chicken, & beef) $5.50-$9.00

o *Jap-Jap* – Calle F, El Cangrejo (This is a Panamanian restaurant – not Japanese – in spite of its politically incorrect name) Grilled chicken, chorizo hot dogs, tamales, & much, much more. Really low prices. Two people can eat for less than $8.00 – a great food bargain and fun!

o *Café Barko* – Isla Flamenco Calzada de Amador is at the end of the causeway with a great view of the city. Specialty: Ceviche. Fun nightlife and very popular with locals. Almost a must!

o *Mi Ranchito* – Amador, L-01 On the Amador causeway. Dining *al fresco* under a *palapa* (thatched roof hut). Excellent food, always crowded.

o ***Restaurante Mercado del Marisco*** – Avenida Balboa, Calle 15. On the second floor of the local seafood market. Really fresh seafood, reasonably priced. Very casual and very good. Modest prices.

- ## Spanish

    o ***Café La Plaza*** – Casco Viejo, next to the Cathedral. Open from 6 PM until early morning. Mostly a place to drink and party. Several varieties of Sangria. Excellent Spanish *topas.*

- ## Steaks

    o ***Martin Fierro*** – Calle Eusebio A Morales. Imported, aged beef. New York strips $16. Local beef, (*bife chorizo*) not as tender, but very tasty $9.50. All their beef is outstanding. Prices include salad and potato. Open noon to 3PM and 6PM to 11PM. Walking distance to Granada, Coral Suites, and Sevilla Suites.

o **_Gauchos Steak House_** – Calle
  Uruguay and Avenida 5 A Sur.
  Excellent steak house. Dinner for
  two with wine about $60.

- ## Argentinean

  o **_Restaurante Los Años Locos_** –
    Grilled Argentinean food. Well
    prepared. Dinner for two about $25.
    Upscale and intimate restaurant.
    Excellent food. Near Hotel Caesar
    Park on Calle 76 Este.

- ## Chinese

  o **_Madame Chang Restaurante Bar_** –
    Calles 48, Bella Vista and Aquillano
    de La Guardia. Outstanding
    Chinese food. Elegant, dressy, and
    really good. Excellent wine list &
    décor. Dinner for two with wine
    about $50.

  o **_Palacio Ling Fung_** – On Calle 62
    Oeste   Very large restaurant with
    outstanding Chinese cuisine. Well-
    priced from $9.50. Dim sung
    served daily until 11 AM. Good
    food, nicely served. A bargain.

71

- **French**

  - ***Restaurante Casco Viejo*** – Calle 53 Este at Calle 50. Excellent French cuisine. Open Monday through Friday, lunch and dinner. Saturday, dinner only. About $40 – dinner for two.

  - ***La Cocotte – 138 Calle Uruguay.*** Lovely nouvelle cuisine. Excellent service. Closed Sundays. $30-$40 for two.

  - ***Crepes & Waffles*** – on Avenida 5B Sur west of Calle Aquilino de la Guardia. Very popular because it's very good. Fine selection of crepes, sandwiches, and desserts. Modest prices from $3.75 to $5.75. Open daily noon to 11 PM.

- **Italian**

  - ***Restaurante de las Americas*** – Calle 57 Este near Avenida 1 Sur. Award winning food. Dressy and moderately expensive, but deserving of its awards. Entrees from $9-$15. They have a 'take-out' place around

the corner where prices are
substantially less.

o *The Wine Bar* – on the ground floor
of Las Vegas Suites Hotel. Open 5
PM – 1 AM. Extremely popular.
Extensive menu of appetizers, and
entrees. Daily pasta specials about
$9.00. Individual pizzas about
$4.00. Live jazz in the evenings.

o *Pizzaria Solemio* On Calle
Uruguay. Closed Monday. Open
11-3 and 6 Pm to 11 PM. Very
good thin crust pizza from a wood-
fired oven. Also, good selection of
pasta and fish. About $7.00 for a
medium pizza.

o *Cafeteria Manolo.* Calle D and
Calle 49 B Oeste. Good Italian
food. Reasonably priced, copious
dinners about $8, full bar with
indoor and outdoor seating.
Pleasant and fun people-watching.

If a restaurant is not listed, it doesn't mean it is lesser
in quality. These are simply a representation of a few
of the many outstanding eateries around the city.

Tipping: The usual percentage is 10-15%.

And don't forget, if you have a **_Pensionado Visa_**, these prices may be reduced by 25%.

Nightlife

Panama's sunsets are spectacular. Their beauty marks the end of beautiful days and the beginning of fun-filled evenings. There is a broad spectrum of things to enjoy in Panama after dark: movies, concerts, casinos, dancing, and the bar-discotheques.

Movies are first-run from Hollywood and generally viewed in the original soundtrack with Spanish sub-titles. Adult tickets are $3.75, and if you have the **_Pensionado_** Visa, that price is reduced to $1.75. It's also reduced on Wednesdays, whether you're a _Pensionado_ or not, to $1.75

Panama City has always been noted for its varied night-life. Bars, discotheques, and restaurants are everywhere. "Happy Hours" are a tradition and generally start at 6 PM and last until 8 PM – sometimes longer. Another tradition is "Ladies Night." Usually on Thursdays.

Dancing is almost a national pastime, with the salsa being most popular, followed closely by merengue, 'rock'n'roll,' and reggae.

Villegas   Bucaneros Night Club

A word about dress attire: you won't be allowed in most clubs if you're not properly dressed. As a minimum, slacks and a shirt with collar to be safe. Many places require a suit or sport coat with ties. Panamanians are less casual than other warm climes in the world – certainly than the dress common in Florida or California. No jeans, short-shorts, or sandals in the evenings at the nicer places.

Most ladies wear a dress with pumps in the evening. It's part of the Panamanian's lives to be a little more formal, and it may go a little deeper into the national psyche. Panama is a tropical country, and it would be very easy to start being casual about everything, starting with the dress code. But they haven't. It's refreshing. Almost like the '50's in the U.S. And it's great to watch people having so much fun.

A tip: if you're going out clubbing, dancing, and drinking, take a taxi!

Salsa & Merengue

- ***Restaurante Casco Viejo***   Calle 53 Este and Calle 50. This elegant French restaurant and popular bar features

- live music – usually salsa or meringue every Friday night. Cover charge or $10.

- ***Hotel Plaza Paitilla Inn***   Via Italia at Avenida Churchill Tuesday and Saturday Nights, a group of talented Cuban musicians and dancers put on a great show, starting at 10 PM. Cover charge of $10.

Many hotel bars have live salsa groups. Caesar Park, El Panama, Hotel Paitilla Inn are just some. Ask a taxi driver for the most current popular clubs.

Rock

- ***Señor Frog's***   Avenida 5A Sur   Live music Wednesday, Thursday & Saturday nights. Similar to all Señor Frogs from Mazatlan to San Jose. Loud, raucous, with the standard Mexican-American décor. Cover $7. Wildly popular.

- **_Skap_**   Down the street from Señor Frogs. Loud and popular. Live music weekends. Cover $10.

- **_Café Dali_**   Calle 5B Sur   Large dance floor, long wooden bar. This is an upscale club. Could be in LA or New York. Live music Fridays only. Very upscale club. Cover of $10 includes two drinks.

- **_Mango's_** On Calle Uruguay Great restaurant by day, with live bands Thursday, Friday, & Saturday evenings. Cover charge: $8.

Jazz

- **_Restaurante Las Bovedos_**   Plaza de Francia in Casco Viejo A former dungeon, great jazz. Tables arranged intimately in alcoves. Atmosphere is terrific. Music on Friday and Saturday nights only.

- **_Mi Rincon_**   Lobby floor of Caesar Park Hotel. Calle 77 Este, one block from the bay. Jazz only on Wednesday nights. Very intimate and posh. No cover.

Casinos

The following hotels have Casinos. They're not as posh as Las Vegas, Atlantic City, or even

San Juan, Puerto Rico, but they all play the same
games of chance and can be fun.

- Hotel Caesar Park
- Hotel Granada
- Miramar-Intercontinental
- Hotel El Panama
- Gran Hotel Soloy
- Hotel Plaza Paitilla Inn

Sight Seeing in Panama City

- **The Canal**

    Once considered the eighth 'wonder of
    the modern world,' the final construction
    was completed in 1914. From that date
    until 1999, the Canal was operated by the
    United States under a treaty with The
    Republic of Panama.

    The Republic of Panama has taken over
    the complete operation of the Canal and all
    properties after President Jimmy Carter
    negotiated and signed the Treaty.

Hutchings   Container Ship   Miraflores Locks

The Canal served both countries' national interests until the end of the twentieth century, and still offers transit to huge number of ships passing from the Atlantic to the Pacific.

Tours are available and you should not miss one – even if your stay in Panama is short. Visitors can go to the Miraflores Locks on the Pacific side 9 AM to 5 PM. A pavilion provides a good vantage point to watch and photograph the ships as they make their transit.

The Canal Train Trip

This is a great trip. It travels a route that parallels the waterway. Some of the tracks are laid along the trail used by the Spanish in the 16th century to carry gold from the Pacific to the Atlantic.

The railroad was the predecessor of the Canal, and was completed in 1855. When gold was discovered in California in 1849, the trip around Cape Horn was long and treacherous. The railroad provided the link from the Atlantic to the Pacific and reduced the dangers and the time of the treacherous voyage – in both directions.

Operated by the U.S. government, it served to transport people, goods, and gold across the Isthmus until 1979. The Panamanian government succeeded the U.S. and operated it until 1998, when service was terminated, and the government sought bids for a private concession. The contract was awarded to a consortium from Chicago who proceeded to spend more than $60-million on a renovation.

The passenger cars are ex-Amtrak units completely rebuilt and refurbished. Coach walls are wood-paneled, carpeting is plush, and the seats very comfortable. (Reminiscent of the Orient Express).

- o The round-trip fare is $30, and the trip takes one hour each way. Obviously, there has to be a better economic reason to spend $60 million than to collect $30-dollar fares. The containerization of ocean shipping is the answer. Containers are off-loaded on one side of the Canal, placed on the railroad, and transported to the other side of the Isthmus in one hour. The Canal transit time is twelve hours, and the fees are substantially more than the rail fee. We're coming full-circle to 1855 when the railroad was first constructed – an economical transit of the Isthmus.

Transit fees through the canal vary by the size and tonnage of the vessel, but they are substantial. Ships pay according to their tonnage. The average cargo vessel pays approximately $30,000 per transit. The very large cruise ships will pay an average of $150,000 to make the transit – one way.

Casco Viejo

The wonderful colonial architecture of the old city is preserved, although much of it has fallen into a state of disrepair.

Hutchings   Casco Viejo

Recognizing its visual and historic appeal, the government is offering some excellent incentives to attract investors to recoup this beautiful and romantic area. (see Business Opportunities)

Stroll the cobblestone streets, have an alfresco lunch at one of the many delightful restaurants, and watch the world pass by.

Hutchings   Casco Viejo

The charm of a renovated Casco Viejo is almost irresistible. It will be a few years before the rebuilding can match that of Cartagena, Colombia, but the wait will be worth it.

Hutchings   Casco Viejo   French Embassy

Historic Panama

o   Panama City was founded in 1519 (on the Pacific side of the isthmus) by a cruel Spanish tyrant, Pedro Arias de Avila. The ruins of this initial settlement can be seen today, known as Panama La Vieja. The city became the focus for Peruvian gold brought by ship to Panama. It was then off-loaded and transported by mule *conductas* across the Camino Real (King's Highway) from Panama City to Portobello on the Atlantic side. The treasures were held at the counting house in Portobello luring Spanish galleons with European goods for trade.

The concentration of this treasure led to it being targeted by English, French, and Dutch pirates and buccaneers. The Spanish fortified Portobello, but in 1671, Henry Morgan, an English pirate, overpowered the Spanish fortifications and marched his small army of pirates across the isthmus. He sacked and burned Panama City – some ruins are still standing.

Marni   Historic Panama Ruins

Morgan loaded 200 mules with the
stolen treasure and returned across he
isthmus to his ships on the Caribbean
side. Morgan was knighted for his
efforts.

• In 1739, the British destroyed Portobello,
   which forced Spain to abandon the Isthmus
   crossing and sail its ships from Spain across
   the Atlantic and around Cape Horn to reach
   the western coast of South America.
   Panama became less important to Spain,
   and eventually came under the control of
   what is now Colombia.

Present Day Panama

   Casco Viejo is still an important part of present day
Panama City. The beautiful colonial buildings,
cathedrals, government offices, and *parques* still stand,
but in various stages of disrepair. The government is
offering substantial incentives for investors to purchase
and modernize these wonderful structures. More on
that in the Business Opportunities section.

   • **Museums, Galleries & Cathedrals**

      If Panama has a weak point, it's in their
   museums. All descriptions are in Spanish, but
   English-speaking guides are available. Tip $3
   or $5 dollars to the guide. It's worth it.

Hutchings   Simon Bolivar Statue

Choose **Panama . . .**

The best overview of Panamanian culture is found in the Museum of the Panamanian, in downtown Panama City. Its collection documents the evolution of human life on the isthmus from the earliest native settlements to the present. Other cultural institutions (all in Panama City) include the Museum of Panamanian History, the Museum of Natural Sciences, the Museum of Religious Colonial Art, the Museum of Contemporary Art, the Museum of the Interoceanic Canal, and the national institutes of culture and music.

- **Museo Antropológicol – Reina de Arauz**

  (Anthtopological Museum) Named after the country's most distinguished anthhtopologist. This museum is in the old railway station on Avenida Central near Plaza Cinco de Mayo. Open Tuesday through Sunday, 9:30 am-4 pm. This is a <u>must-see</u> museum. Represented are many pre-Columbian artifacts and a well documented history of the Panamanian people.

- **Museo of Ciencias Naturales** (Museum of Natural Sciences) – Open 9am to 4pm Tuesday through Saturday. This Museum has very interesting sections on geology, paleontology, entomology, and marine biology. Wonderful taxidermy of many of the isthmus' wild, exotic creatures.

Museo del Canal Interoceánico (Museum of the Interoceanic Canal)
This is a terrific exhibition housed in a beautiful French Colonial Building. Opened in 1997 with varied display of Spanish armor, artifacts from the gold rush days, paintings, photos, and many canal railroad and canal construction exhibits. English speaking guides if you call ahead. (211-1650) @ Plaza de la Indepencia in Casco Viejo. $2 fee.

There are several other museums you'll find listed in guide books, but these three are by far the most interesting and well-displayed.

The Parks

- **Parque Natural Metropolitano**

  This wonderful 265 hectare (about 540 acres) park is located north of downtown and comprises a wild, tropical rain forest within the city limits. There are two walking trails: The Nature Trail and the Titi Monkey Trail. They combine to form a loop leading to a *mirador* (lookout point) which overlooks the city, the canal, and the bay.

Mammals residing here include anteaters, white-tail deer, sloths, and marmosets. There are more than 250 species of birds in the park.

The park is also home to the Smithsonian Tropical Research Institute. There's a nice visitor center, and Park rangers offer a one hour tour and slide show for a fee of $5 to groups of five or more.

The Panama Audubon Society holds a monthly meeting at the Visitor Center on the second Thursday of every month from 7:30pm to 9:30pm and these meetings are open to the public.

Sobernia National Park

This a very large natural rainforest and jungle. Please use professional guides when visiting Sobernia. This is a jungle, and one could get lost.

Birders from the all over the world visit the area known as "pipeline road." This trail is legendary. More than 500 species of birds are known to use this habitat.

One of the nicest, though 'pricey,' ways to see this fabulous area is to stay at the $30-million Gamboa Rainforest Resort. This is a fantastic adventure, with 110 guestrooms, nicely appointed.

One of their tour-inclusive packages is $675 for four nights (double occupancy), includes breakfast, a sunrise birding tour on Pipeline Road, a morning boat tour of Lago Gatun, a ride on the aerial tram through the rain forest canopy, unlimited use of kayaks and paddle boats, bicycles, gym, tennis courts, and unlimited access to all of the exhibits – including the butterfly and snake farm.

Getting Around

Rental Cars are available at the airports and in several locations in Panama City. A valid driver's license is all that is required. In Panama City, one other thing is a necessity. ***Courage.*** For the uninitiated, driving in the city can be an adventure, at the very least.

There is a lack of traffic lights, street signs, and traffic police. There is an abundance of really poor local drivers – who also are fearless. Driving here is much like driving in Mexico City, except there isn't the mind-bending congestion or smog.

Buses, taxis, motor scooters, and cars make up the vehicular population. Some of which are driven like *Via Espana* was on the NASCAR circuit. To get around the city, please take a cab or a bus.

This emphasizes a point. Americans are car-crazy and car-dependent. Do you really need to own a car in Panama? Whether you live in the city, the beach, or in the mountains, taxis are cheap. Really cheap. Buses even cheaper. Buses are frequent and can take you anywhere in the city. Or the country.

Hutchings   Panama City Bus

Intercity buses are ultra-modern and luxurious. And, they're inexpensive. For instance, bus fare to David, a city on the Pacific coast 250 miles northwest of Panama City, is $15. The vehicle is an air-conditioned luxury bus that shows movies, has toilet facilities, the seats are reserved, and it has an attendant who serves refreshments. (No chickens or goats!) Of course, if you're in a hurry to get to David, you can fly for $57. – about one hour.

If you are vacationing, why not relax and enjoy the trip. If you're going to retire here, you may not wish to bother with the expense of a car. Perhaps, the purchase price of a car is better spent buying or renting a nicer home. And, you'll not have the expense of maintaining and operating the vehicle. No car insurance, no title or registration fees, and none of the associated repairs.

You can take a taxi to the store for a dollar. You can take the bus to the store for fifteen cents. And, on the bus, you'll begin to know and appreciate the people – and vice versa.

Airlines

The following Airlines serve Panama from the United States. U.S. cities served are: Los Angeles, Miami, Orlando, Houston, New York, Newark, NJ, Washington, DC, and Dallas. Some flights are non-stop. Others may make stops in Mexico City, Managua, Guatemala City, or San Jose, Costa Rica.

American Airlines	800-433-7300
Continental Airlines	800-231-0856
COPA	800-25-2272
Delta Airlines	800-221-4141
EVA	800-695-1188
Lacsa	800-225-2272
Mexicana	800-531-7921
TACA	800-225-2272
United Airlines	800-241-6522

Typical coach fares* (Round Trip) and flight time (Non-Stop):

City	Fare	Flite Time
Los Angeles, CA	$410	6 hrs
Houston, TX	$395	4.5 hrs
Washington, DC	$446.	5 hrs
Newark, NJ	$456.	5 hrs.
New York, NY	$452.	5 hrs.
Miami, FL	$316.	2.5 hrs

* Obviously, fares are subject to change. These fares prevailed in early 2004. All flight times are non-stop. If your flight makes one stop (with layover), add at least 2 hours to the total flight time. Sometimes, a premium is charged for non-stop flights.

Tocumen International Airport is about 20 miles from Panama City. Taxis to the heart of the city are officially $25, but there are alternatives. You could share a cab with a fellow passenger. Some hotels have shuttles - free. And, there are regular buses to the downtown and business districts.

Entertainment & Recreation

Golf and Tennis

The **Summit Golf and Resort** is a world-class golf and country club. It was originally opened during World War II for American employees of the Canal and military officers. The club is less than thirty minutes from the city. The course is of championship caliber – touted by World Golf as the best course in Central America.

Facilities include a bar, dining room, pool, tennis, and squash. Memberships are less than $5,000. There are no greens fees for members, and monthly dues are $135. This is a private club, but is open to the public. Green fees, including a cart are $90. for tourists and $40. for residents.

The **Coronado Hotel and Resort** is 52 miles west of Panama City. It has a 7,000 yard course designed by George Fazio. This is a complete resort with an Equestrian Club, Spa, Tennis, Bar, & Restaurants. The resort has 75 suites and is located on a lovely Pacific beach. Call 264-2863 for fees and tee reservations.

If you're in Boquete, there's a nice nine hole course at the **Quebrado Golf and Country Club** located at Valle Escondido. The course winds through an active coffee plantation and is quite beautiful, with bent grass greens.

A new 18-hole course is scheduled to open near Boquete in the Spring of 2006. See section on Boquete.

Fishing

The indigenous meaning of Panama is "abundant fish." It is a fact that more world records are held for fish caught in Panamanian waters than anywhere else in the world. Black Marlin, Blue Marlin, Blackfin Tuna, Roosterfish, Wahoo, Sailfish, Dorado, Pompano – and the list goes on.

One of the more popular charter fishing companies is *Pesca Panama.* Check out their website at www.pescapanama.com They are located out of David and offer great fishing near Coiba Island.

World famous for more than 200 world class records is *Tropic Star Lodge in* Pinas Bay. Fish the incomparable Zane Grey reef for the ultimate deep sea experience. www.tropicstar.com

Panama Yacht Tours specialize in trips to the Pearl Islands and Isla Coiba for sport fishing, snorkeling, diving, and Panama Canal Transits. www.panamatours.com

In addition, there is wonderful fly fishing for rainbow trout in the mountain streams of Chiriqui province on the Rio Caldera and Rio Chiriqui.   So if you enjoy fishing, either fresh or saltwater, Panama holds a lot of adventure in store for you.

Birding

Panama is home to approximately 950 species of birds – more than the total of species found in all the rest of North America.

Birders are more likely to see the rare and beautiful Quetzal here than anywhere in the world. Although this resplendent creature is the national bird of Costa Rica, it is far more abundant in Panama, and is seen regularly here rather than being that rare sighting in Costa Rica.

The top birding spots are easily accessible. The world famous "Pipeline Road" in the old canal zone is only 45 minutes from Panama City, as is the Canopy Tower. Other prime locations are Boquete, Bambito, Cerro Punta, and Volcan in the Chiriqui Highlands of West Panama. Eco and Birding guides are readily available in all of these locations. Except for Boquete and Volcan, the other villages are primarily inhabited by the colorful and friendly natives of the Ngobe-Buglé tribe.

Many people choose to combine the gourmet coffee farm tours with their bird watching and hiking. (See the section on 'Western Highlands) Mt. Baru, an extinct volcano, is Panama's highest peak at over

11,400 feet. If you're up to the hike, both Atlantic and Pacific oceans can be seen from the top of Mt. Baru. The hike will also reward you with wild orchids, waterfalls, and of course, many, many bird sightings. A good starting point for one of these expeditions is the charming village of Boquete.

Hiking

The rain forests of Panama offer an unparalleled opportunity for eco-hikes. Even the parks and forests near and in Panama City are abundant in flora and fauna.

A word of caution: taking off into these rain forests should not be done without hiring a qualified guide.

These are wild, primitive areas of forest and jungle. Besides the monkeys, birds, orchids, etc., there are jaguars, pumas, and snakes – not to mention the possibility of twisting an ankle or some other injury.

Sailing, Diving, and Surfing

There is a fine yacht club near the end of the Amador Causeway. Panama is a great sailing area and is a frequent destination of both Caribbean and Pacific sailors. Panama Bay offers wonderful day sailing. The entrance to the Canal, and views of the City's exciting skyline are dramatic sights.

Hutchings   Yacht Club

The Pearl Islands (where many of the 'Survivor' TV series were shot), Tobaga and Contadero Islands are great sailing destinations.

On the Caribbean side, you can visit the **San Blas Islands** with sail tours of 2-14 days. There are more than 350 islands, with wonderful coral reefs to dive and snorkel, and the unique culture of the Kuna Indians who inhabit this archipelago.

As beautiful and interesting as the San Blas Archipelago might be, remember, it is not a choice for retirement. It is mentioned here so that whether retiring to Panama or just visiting, it is one of the highlights you should not miss.

There are more than 1,000 islands to explore off the Panama coasts. And, the waters are pleasantly warm in both the Caribbean and Pacific.

J. Miller   San Blas Beach

Surfing

While surfing is generally reserved for the younger set, some seniors do still enjoy the sport.

Panama has surfing beaches in both the Atlantic and Pacific sides of the Isthmus. On the Atlantic side, Bocas del Toro is a favorite. The best time to surf in Bocas is between December and March. Check with the local surf shops for location and current breaks.

Probably the best conditions are on the Pacific side. Several beaches in Panama Province are excellent. Los Santos Province is probably the best surf in the country although some addicts feel that Veraguas Province has the best surf in Central America.

Chiriqui Province has good surf, but the best is out among the remote off-shore islands. Again, consult with a tour operator.

Photography

Obviously, a country so rich in natural beauty and history grants the photographer a wealth of opportunity.

Certainly, the canal, the rail trip, and the many plazas are places to memorialize with your camera. And, the beaches of Bocas del Toro, the Pearl Islands, and Contadora Island all have the palms and sandy beaches we love.

The San Blas Islands and area offer wonderful photo opportunities not only of pristine beaches and azure waters, but the very interesting lifestyle of the Kuna Indians.

J. Miller   San Blas Beach

The skies over Panama can be truly spectacular. Cloud formations seem to billow forever, highlighted by morning or the setting sun. One can almost imagine Sir Henry Morgan or Sir Francis Drake sailing in from the horizon to their favorite uninhabited places of refuge within the Pearl Islands.

The electronic and camera shops in Panama City stock almost every piece of camera equipment made – at bargain prices – so if you don't have the latest in digital or film technology, don't despair. It's here.

Rafting & Kayaking

In the province of Chiriqui, there is rafting galore with rapids ranging from Class 2 to Class 5, depending on the time of year. They extend to Class VI but the local operators will refuse to run them when they are that dangerous.

Rivers flow from the mountainsides of Volcan Baru and are generally bordered by heavy forest and jungle. There are two rafting and kayak companies located in downtown Boquete. **Chiriqui River Rafting** and **Panama Rafters** both offer trips ranging from family floats to the wild runs of Class IV and Class V rapids.

Panama is generally regarded as one of the top rafting rivers in the world – certainly on a par, if not

better than the Tuolumne River or the Middle Fork of
the American River in California.

The operators of both companies, Hector Sanchez
of **Chiriqui River Rafting** and Kevin Mellinger of
Panama Rafters are highly regarded professionals.

The river environments of Chiriqui province are
wild, wonderful areas. Wildlife is abundant. Monkeys
and parrots screech at your presence. Exotic birds, and
once in a while a big cat – Jaguar or Puma – can be
scene in the jungles as you roar down the rapids.

You can visit www.panama-rafting.com (Chiriqui
River Rafting) or www.panamarafters.com for more
information.

Kayaking has become very popular. The *Rio
Chiriqui* is accessible by two-wheel drive for most of
the runs. The run that drains from Volcan Baru toward
Costa Rica is the premier of Panama's white water
runs. As you transit the river, one gets the feeling of
being miles and miles from civilization. You'll pass
through gorges surrounded by forest and waterfalls
with areas of Class II to Class V water.

People of Panama

Panama's diverse population is approaching
3,000,000. A high percentage of this population is
concentrated along the Panama Canal.

Almost 70% of Panama City's 700,000 residents are either Mestizo (mixed Native American and European background) or Mulatto (mixed European and African heritage). Others are descended from European and Caribbean immigrants who arrived in the 19th and 20th centuries as labor for construction of the Panama Canal.

Approximately ten percent of the population is of European and/or North American descent, while Native Americans account for six percent.

Panama has long served as a crossroads between oceans and continents, and thus has attracted immigrants from all over the world. This diverse population is concentrated in the capital, as well as in other cities such as David (population 130,000) and Santiago (35,000). People from the West Indies, the Middle East, Asia, and North America are now represented in Panama City. Most of the city's residents are Roman Catholic, but Jewish and other religious communities are also present.

William Hutchings

J. Miller   Kuna Woman

Away from the major urban areas, residents are mestizo and Native American. Many of the agricultural workers are Native American. This is especially true in Chiriqui province where they labor in the coffee plantations on the slopes of Mt. Baru.

The principal Native Americans are the Ngobe-Buglé (the largest group) who inhabit the mountains of Chiriqui and the Bocas del Toro region. The Chocó people inhabit the Darién jungle on the Panama and Colombian border, and the Kuna people live in the San Blas Archipelago on the Caribbean coast, east of Colón, in an area known as the Comarca of San Blas.

Most of the indigenous people live apart from the majority of Panamanians. The Kuna interact more than the others, but still maintain and preserve their culture.

Government

Politically, the government of Panama is a democratic republic. The country's official name is: *Republicá de Panamá*. It has well-established democratic traditions since its declaration of independence from Spain in 1821.

The president is the most powerful political figure. The president runs the executive branch and wields a good deal of influence over the legislative and judicial branches of the government. The presidential term is five years, and the president cannot succeed himself. Two elected vice-presidents assist the president.

The Presidential Palace and the legislative buildings are located in Casco Viejo. The legislature is composed of 72 members, who are also elected for a term of five years. Like the president, they cannot succeed themselves.

There are nine provinces, each administered by a presidential appointed governor. Local government is divided into sixty-five districts and 505 sub-districts. Mayors are elected by the local population, and do have significant power.

Marni   Presidential Residence (Las Garzas)

The voting age is 18, and <u>voting is compulsory</u>.

The Native American groups negotiate directly with the national government, and the Kuna enjoy special rights to conduct and administer their own affairs that pertain to their reservation, the Comarca of San Blas.

There is no standing army, and the closest thing to a military organization is the police.

Why no standing army?

First of all, there is a mutual defense pact with the United States. The U.S. is obligated to protect the Republic. Secondly, most standing armies of small countries are not there to protect themselves against invasion. They have been formed to protect the rulers – most generally dictators. Witness the time of Manuel Noriega.

Language and Religion

Panama's official language is Spanish. About 25% of the population speaks English. Some of the Native Americans (Kuna, Chocó, Ngobe-Buglé) prefer to speak their own dialects, not Spanish.

About 80% of Panamanians are Catholic, although the percentage of those who practice Catholicism is somewhat smaller. Protestant denominations account for about 15% of the population.

The constitution of Panama does not specifically separate church and state, but the constitution does guarantee freedom of worship.

There have been no incidents of religious conflict, civil violations, or religious discrimination recorded.

Education

Education of all citizens is provided free through four-year university level. The government budget for schooling is 18% of its expenditures. There are several private schools and a Roman Catholic University. Many of the wealthier students receive their university education in the United States.

Some private schools and trade schools have started up in recent years. With the government's budget for education and their efforts to educate the youth of the country, Panama's literacy rate has reached 97%.

Climate

Panama is in the tropical zone, but cooler temperatures prevail at higher elevations. If it's too warm at sea level, pick the climate of your choice by going higher in elevation for your place to live.

Temperatures in the coastal area range from 85-degrees to 95-degrees, year round. On the mountain slopes, daytime temperatures will average 72-degrees year round, and they cool down substantially at night. In the regions of Boquete or Volcan, a sweater or light jacket will be needed in the evenings. And, you'll sleep under a light blanket.

Because of its proximity to the equator, Panama does not have temperature-defined seasons as we do in temperate zones north of the Tropic of Capricorn, or in South America, south of the Tropic of Cancer. Seasons in Panama are defined as "wet" and "dry."

The "dry" season is December until May. The "wet" season is May through November, with October and November experiencing the heaviest rain. During the "wet" season, the mornings are usually sunny, and by noon, it can begin to get cloudy. One or two afternoon showers are normal. These are usually brief in duration, but can be quite heavy. The rains tend to get heavier toward the end of the wet season, particularly in November and early December. It also rains during the "dry" season, but the rain is less intense and of shorter duration.

The Caribbean (northern) coast receives much more rain than the Pacific (southern) coast or the Western Highlands. Panama City is on the Pacific coast. The average rainfall on the northern coast around Bocas del Toro is about 115-inches per year – most of which falls during the "wet" season.

The Pacific winds hitting the southern coast are drier and consequently, rainfall is substantially less – about 65-inches per year. Again, the bulk of this moisture occurs in the "wet" season.

Panama is located outside the paths of Caribbean and Pacific hurricanes that track several hundred miles to the north, and there are no active volcanoes in the country.

However, Panama is on the western edge of the American Continents. Earthquakes do occur along the Americas from Tierra de Fuego in the south to the Aleutian Islands in the north. Anyone living in the U.S. from California to Alaska can attest to tremors and occasional earthquakes.

It is important to note that one of the primary reasons for choosing the isthmus as the site of the Canal over Nicaragua (the second choice), was the decidedly lower incidence of earthquakes in the isthmus region.

Staying Healthy

No inoculations are required to visit Panama, but it is recommended that all travelers get the series of Hepatitis A and B, Tetanus, and Typhoid before traveling anywhere. This is probably more important in the rest of Central America than in Panama.

The Hepatitis series is taken in a series of three inoculations, which are spaced 30, and 150 days apart. Therefore, try to plan ahead. This is excellent advice for any Caribbean, Central or South American country. The most economical place to receive inoculations is from the County Health Department near your home.

Medical facilities in major cities (Panama City, Santiago, and David) are excellent. Many doctors on the medical staffs have received their training in the U.S. Hospitals are very modern and are equipped with the latest innovations in medical technology. One person has described entering the Paitilla Hospital in Panama City "like walking into the Marriott."

Most communities have a medical clinic with a staff of doctors and nurses. If a serious illness should occur, and the patient or family would like to go back to the states, Miami is only a 2-1/2 hour flight from Panama City.

While visiting Boquete, the author suffered a badly broken leg, and was rushed to the Chiriqui hospital in David, twenty-two miles away. (I slipped on a wet tile floor) The hospital care was excellent, and the orthopedic surgeon did a terrific and professional job. I had a severe helical fracture, and the surgery was complex. The total bill for hospital and surgical care was less than $5,000. After returning to California, I was told the same operation in the States would have been at least seven or eight times that amount.

The nursing staff at Chiriqui was attentive and always responded immediately to my needs. At every shift change, day or night, the nurses would check temperature, blood pressure, and pulse, ask if I was in pain, etc. The staff was wonderful, but the food was like hospital food everywhere.

I suspect that hospital and airline chefs have all attended the same school where they learn how to change the color of meat from red to gray. (It's their form of alchemy)   I lived for breakfast with ham and eggs. Two friends kept me from wasting away to nothing by sneaking in BLT sandwiches.

Medical Insurance

Before visiting any foreign country, check your medical insurance to see if you're covered for emergencies while away from home. It's not uncommon to turn an ankle on a cobblestone street or slip on a glazed tile floor.

While Medicare does not usually provide coverage out of the country, some HMO supplements and PPO's do. Also, check with your travel agent. There are plans available designed for your trip that will give you that extra protection, and they are not terribly expensive.

What about medical insurance in Panama?

It's available, and it's reasonable. The average Panamanian earns a little over $300 per month. And, the doctors and hospitals do not have to pay the outlandish cost of malpractice insurance so pervasive in the U.S. These factors tend to keep the premiums of medical insurance significantly lower.

Choose Panama . . .

Several private insurance plans are available. Many have one thing in common: enrollment must be made by age 59. Once you're enrolled, you can still be covered as long as you pay your premium. However, the premium will rise with age.

One company, Capital de Seguras, S.A., (507-223-1511) allows enrollment up to age 64. Most companies require that you be a resident of Panama for 3 to 5 months. A popular plan for expatriates is offered by British American Tu Seguro Principal (507-269-0515). For age 59 their premium is $59 month for an individual, and $104. for the family.

Two hospitals, San Fernando in Panama City, and Chiriqui Hospital in David have their own plans. Joining these plans is not limited by age at the time of enrollment, and I believe you can enroll up to the age of 80. These plans cover the cost of hospitalization and surgery with a 30% co-pay and a $10,000 maximum annual coverage limitation.

There are some exclusions or waiting periods for pre-existing conditions, as in most insurance plans. Cost rises with age, but a 65 year old is looking at a monthly premium of about $50 at Chiriqui.

The important thing is that coverage is available. Medical care is excellent, and if you prefer to be seen in the states, remember, it is only a 2-1/2 hour flight from Panama City to Miami.

Personal Safety

Pinkerton Global Intelligence Agency, the world-renowned security firm, has given Panama its highest rating for tourist security. Panama has a low rate of violent crime and is one of the four safest places to reside in the world. Much safer than Mexico or Costa Rica.

Since turning the Canal over to Panama, relations with the U.S. and Panama have improved dramatically. Citizens of the U.S. are welcomed by the government and by the people of Panama.

Places to Avoid

Although Panama is generally quite safe, and the incidence of violent crime is very low, there are places to take caution, just as you would in Miami, Chicago, Los Angeles, or New York.

I had a friend mugged by two women in New York just outside the Hilton Hotel on Avenue of the Americas. Flamboyant displays of jewelry, fat wallets, flashing of cash, etc., should be avoided wherever you travel in the entire world.   Use common sense.

After dark, always take a cab – especially if you're club-hopping in Casco Viejo. It's not like going to South Central in LA, the Bedford-Stuyvesant in New York, or certain areas in Miami, but caution is always best.

The usual concerns about petty theft should always be observed. Pickpockets and purse-snatchers have been around since pockets and purses were invented. Colon, on the Atlantic side, is much more of a concern than Panama City.

Truly dangerous is the area known as the Darien Gap. This is the dense jungle along the Panamanian-Columbian border. There are simply too many great places to go in Panama other than the Darien Gap. Even the Pan-American highway stops here. The area is infested with thugs and bandits. Several backpackers have been missing after attempting to penetrate this jungle. It's best to avoid it.

Banking

The skyscrapers, palm-lined boulevards, and the modernity of Panama City are truly eye openers. Almost one hundred banks populate the financial district. Tall, solid looking structures of glass and steel are everywhere. Not the brass plaque "banks" you find in front of a lawyer's office on Caribbean islands. These are real banks with vaults, tellers, safety deposit boxes, wire services, etc.

It is not easy to open a Panamanian bank account unless you have obtained a permanent visa. Since Noriega's capture, the banking system has been revised. The country is particularly sensitive to elements that may have some connection with drugs or organized crime.

Panama has made a concerted effort to become one of the most modern banking centers in the world. Their laws encourage privacy and restrict the invasive access by governments of all nations. They do have numbered accounts, and bearer bonds are legal. But the banks are terribly conscious of attempted illegal "laundering" of monies and deposits by criminal elements. In many respects, Panama has "out-swissed" the Swiss.

To open a bank account, you will need reference letter(s) from your current bank(s).

Hutchings   Financial Area – Panama City

Real Estate

Foreigners are permitted to own property anywhere in Panama except within 3.7 miles of a national border. Foreigners have the same property rights as citizens.

Real Estate Taxes

1. All land and improvements thereon located in Panama are subject to Real Estate tax.

2. Real Estate is appraised by an Agency of the Ministry of Economy and Finances. The taxable base is determined by the total value of the land and all improvements.

3. Real Estate transactions at prices above the appraisal automatically increase the value of such properties for tax purposes

4. Certain properties or improvements are exempt or can be qualified for exemption according to special incentive tax laws. (see visa incentives)

5. Real estate properties with assessed value of less than $20,000 are exempt from taxes.

6. Real Estate taxes have priority over any other encumbrances

7. Taxes can be paid in three installments:
    April 30, Aug 31, and Dec 31.

8. A Tax Clearance Certificate <u>must</u> be
    obtained before any Real Estate transaction
    can be completed.

    <u>It is highly</u> recommended you hire an
    attorney for any real estate transaction.
    Property in most areas can be purchased
    legally and safely. (In Bocas del Toro there
    are some special circumstances. Be very
    careful in Bocas)

9.   Once you've found a property and you
    want to make an offer to buy, (and the
    Seller wants to sell) the owner <u>must</u> give
    you three vital documents that your
    attorney will need:

    a) The *Escritura* (The Title & Public
    Deed):

    b) *The Certificado de Registro Publico*
    (Ownership and Encumbrances
    Certificate) These documents are
    available from the Public Registry.

    c) The *finca* number

10. With these documents and their
    information, your attorney can perform

a title search. (Very similar to a Title and Abstract search in the United States) <u>These documents must be originals</u> and bear the stamps, signatures, and seals of the Registration Office. The seller must provide the survey plans of the property with a description of all buildings, their size, and location on the property. (Very similar to a plot map in the U.S.)

11. Enter into a purchase contract with the Seller. Your attorney will draft this. Upon signing, a down payment is required. Normally the agreement provides for liquidated damages should either party default, and a closing date is established for the transfer of title. The attorney should make a complete search at this point for any liens or encumbrances on the property. The seller normally pays the transfer taxes and obtains the clearance certificates required for title transfer. The buyer arranges payment (cash or financing) and at the stated closing date, Buyer and Seller sign the final contract.

12. The attorney will formalize the final contract and draw up a public deed. The attorney(s), Buyer and Seller take the documents to a Notary Public for

signing and authentication. Notary Publics in Panama (actually, in all Napoleonic Code countries) are significantly important. They are more important to the transaction than in Common Law countries and are considered high ranking officials. Like escrow officers, they are strictly neutral and represent neither Buyer nor Seller.

13. The attorney will assist in transferring final payment. One of the safest ways to transfer the funds is through an irrevocable letter of payment from your bank. This letter will promise to pay the seller the final amount due upon the recording of the new title. In this way, the Buyer avoids the risk of payment if for whatever reason title is not properly recorded.

14. It is highly recommended you have your attorney follow through with the recording at the main office of Public Registry in Panama City. The normal time for final recording is a few weeks. However, for costs of about $250 this time can be cut to ten days. <u>Consult with your attorney.</u>

There are certain areas in the country where titles can be a gray area. Never try to buy

property in the San Blas region. The Kuna
Indians have been granted sovereignty in
this area. The Kunas are dedicated to
maintaining their present way of life, and
would unequivocally refuse to sell one
grain of sand or one coconut tree to any
one.

Around Bocas del Toro, most of the land is
owned by the Panamanian government, so
it is not legal for a foreigner to buy – at
least not until it has been first owned by a
Panamanian. (This restriction only applies
to land not previously owned and titled by a
Panamanian citizen)

There are also problems with possessory
rights in Bocas, as well as squatter's rights
in this area. You might buy a property,
think all is well, and wake up some
morning to find a native sitting in your back
yard claiming it's his home. Another
nightmare.

Panamanian Labor Laws

One of the joys of moving to Panama is the
abundance and quality, of good labor. Generally, the
people are kind and of good humor. There are
exceptions as in any generalization, but I don't believe
I've ever encountered people of such grace and work
ethic. They are scrupulously clean and detailed in their

assignments. The Panamanians are lovely people, diligent, and very hardworking.

However, Panamanian labor laws apply to all of them. It is important that you understand the law and the government's paternalistic attitude. The government will not allow their people to be taken advantage of – in any way. The doctrine is best expressed in Latin:

"In Dubio Pro Operario"

Simply stated, if there be a labor dispute, the burden of proof lies with the employer. The **employee** is <u>always</u> right unless the **employer** can prove otherwise.

So, what can we learn from this?

- **Never** hire anyone - whether maid, part-time maid, gardener, or a handyman without recording a signed agreement in writing – in Spanish and English. The operative word here is **"NEVER."**

- Understand and recognize the different types of contracts according to Panamanian law:

    o A specific period of time contract
    o A non-specific period of time contract

o A specific work contract (plumber,
builder, etc.)

*The labor rates are so affordable, that we
should never try to take advantage of the workers.*

This can be a confusing subject for newcomers.
To give an example of possible liabilities unless
you protect yourself: you hire a maid to work for
three hours a day, three days a week. She is the
best maid you could possibly imagine. Three
months into her employment, she becomes
pregnant.

*You might be liable for her medical care, her
child's medical care, the child's up-bringing and
schooling, etc., etc.*

So, what can you do to prevent this calamity?
As in Real Estate, consult a good Panamanian
attorney before hiring. We talked with Lea del
Adames Franceschi in David. (507) 774-4426 of
Burbano y Adames, Abogadas (Attorneys).

Lea is fluent in English and is very conversant
in Real Estate and Labor law. A short consultation
with her on domestic labor law will cost about $50.
Tell her what you want, and she will draft a
contract to cover your needs. Save yourself a lot of
potential headache. (She's an absolute **MUST** on
real estate transactions where 'possessory rights'
are involved.)

123

The laws are different in Panama. Don't think of the norm in your home country and believe that it might apply here. It probably doesn't.

Real Estate Around Panama City

When 50,000 Americans left Panama in December 2000, it left a deep hole in the real estate market in and around Panama City. The Panamanian government took over all of the military bases and buildings including the military housing. Officer's quarters, enlisted barracks, and of course, everything the United States had established in the "zone," including some very impressive housing.

It's important to reiterate that in Panama, foreigners have the same rights as citizens to own property.

It's also important to understand the author is not in the real estate business and has no interest whatsoever in any properties mentioned in this book. For you to determine whether or not Panama is within your budget, examples are simply given so that you will have an idea on what to expect. Or at least, what prices and availability were in early 2004.

The Panamanian government has been auctioning or selling much of the real estate formerly held by the United States in the Canal Zone and on military bases to private citizens and investors. Although quite a bit has been sold, there's a significant amount still available.

For example, there are four-plexes, containing 1,200 square feet in each unit, which are currently being sold for less than $140,000. That's approximately $30 per square foot. These were all built to U.S. standards for the U.S. government. Some buildings need work since they've been empty for four years, but those representative prices warrant investigation as a potential for rental income units.

There are new condominiums in the city that are also bargains. A new 2 bedroom, 2 bath condo containing approximately 900 square feet was recently purchased for $57,000. This apartment has a balcony and beautiful view. It is air-conditioned, and in a full-service high-rise building in an up-scale neighborhood of Panama City.

If you have a significant budget, there are 3,000 square foot high-luxury apartments available that may cost as much as $250,000 to $300,000. Obviously, there is a lot of available real estate between $50,000 and $300,000. If urban living is your choice, there are excellent values available.

Listed below are a few representative apartment and single-family residence prices in Panama City. Most have separate maid quarters.

Apartments – Panama City - New

Name	Sq. Ft.	Price	BR	BA	Pool	Md	Sec
Torre Vista Marina	3583	$ 396,000	3	4.5	●	●	●
Ocean Park	2690	234,000	3	4.5	●	●	●
Victoria Tower	2173	170,000	3	3	●	●	●
Long Beach	2184	159,000	3	3.5	●	●	●
Mystic Point	1588	126,500	3	3.5	●	●	●
Aurora Tower	1713	110,000	3	2.5	●	●	●
Brisas del Carmen	1312	86,000	3	2	●	●	●
Porto Vita	1080	62,500	2	2	●	●	●
Mirador	846	57,800	2	2	●	●	●
Parque de Versailles	900	47,750	3	2			

These are just a few examples to give you a broad spectrum of availability and prices of **new** apartments in the city (at the time of this writing), and these examples are not intended to be recommended above any others.

Obviously, prices and availability will change, and there are many existing vacancies not listed.

Single Family Residences (new)

Project Name	Sq. Ft.	Price	BR	BA	Pool
Costa dl Perlas	3554	$ 311,000	3	3	
Albrook Garden	2720	198,500	3	3	
Costa Bay	3362	158,700	3	2.5	
Brisa de Viscaya	2110	116,750	3	2.5	
Coronado Equestre	600	81,250	2	1	●
Dorado Lakes	1613	72,500	3	3	
Princessa de Gales	2840	59,700	3	2	
San Remo	1452	45,000	3	2	

Again, these are just a few of the developments available, and are not to be construed as recommendations. And, these are all new developments. The resale market offers a far wider choice.

Island Living

There are nearly 1,000 islands off both coasts of Panama. Several of these offer a wonderful opportunity to enjoy one's dream. The Caribbean coast differs greatly from the Pacific coast, so we'll look at the pros and cons of each area.

Remember, our perspective is to view these options as places of prospective retirement – not as vacation destinations .

127

They might be an excellent investment, and/or great vacation spots once you've moved here.

• *Bocas del Toro – Caribbean Side*

Interpreted literally, *Bocas del Toro* means Mouth of the Bull. If you check the maps of the region, it is easy see how well the name fits.

Marni   Bocas Beach

For years, this area was the principal headquarters and export area for the famous *Chiquita* bananas of the United Fruit Company. In the late thirties, a local banana blight radically reduced the operations in the area. Because of its beauty and tranquility, Bocas began developing as a prime tourist attraction.

Bocas (The Town) is about 10 hours driving time from Panama City via David, and about a 55 minute flight from the Albrook airport. It's only a half hour flight from David, and is one of Panama's top tourist attractions.

Marni   Bocas Bar

The town of Bocas is 'quaint,' with a permanent population of approximately 4,000. The Jamaican descendents usually speak some form of English. The Latins speak mostly Spanish.

Accommodations in town (Bocas Town) are increasing.

Marni   Quaint Restaurant (Bocas)

The town is located on the island of Colon, the largest island in the group, and is the seat of government for the province. (Don't confuse this with the city of Colon at the Atlantic entrance to the Canal.)

There are few autos on the island and not many full-time gringos. Its nightlife can be hectic at times with the many young people who love to come here. Salsa and Carib-Afro music dominate the dancing.

Hospedaje Heike on Calle 3 near the center of town was rebuilt in 2001. It has seven rooms with ceiling fans, mosquito nets and two shared bathrooms (with hot water) ranging from $5 - $15 per night. This is a good value.

Marni   Bocas Town

Several other small, quaint hotels offer similar facilities in town: *Hospedaje Emmanuel, Hospedaje EYL, Hotel Las Brisas, Hotel Casa Max, Hotel Angela.* These are all small hotels of six to eight rooms.

Others, more mid-range are: *Hotel Dos Palmas, Hotel La Veranda,* and the older, stately hotel built by United Fruit in 1905, *Hotel Bahia – at $35-40 per night.* All rooms are air conditioned, with private hot-water baths. Some have balconies and ocean views. (507) 676-4669

Upscale facilities include: *The Bocas Inn,* (507-269-9414) 12 lovely air-conditioned rooms, including breakfast, ranging from $40-60. There is a restaurant and bar. www.anconexpeditions.com

131

Cocomo on the Sea, small but attractive seaside inn (4 rooms). Nicely decorated. No pets or children under eight. Rates are $45 including breakfast. On *Calle H*. www.panamainfo.com/cocomo

Another nice resort is *Punta Caracol* (507-676-7186) whose 2-story Cabins are on stilts, built over a coral reef, so diving is easy. And great. About 20 minutes from town, and far enough away from the mangrove swamps to minimize the no-see-ums and mosquitoes. Price is $100/couple including breakfast. Beautiful restaurant is excellent. www.puntacaracol.com

Marni   Bocas Hotel

Bocas is typical Caribbean beauty, charm, and quaintness. Most of the beaches are beautiful.

Marni   Bocas Beach

There are also the mangrove swamps that harbor lots of 'no-see-ums' and mosquitoes.

It's a place not too different from what you'll find on many of the islands of the Caribbean. Stunning beaches, palm trees, and warm azure waters teeming with the color of tropical fish.

Homes in Bocas vary from older, dilapidated places you wouldn't choose to own to newer, modern residences you'd love to own.

Marni   Dilapidated Water Front

Prices of Bocas waterfront property can be almost beyond belief. Even for rundown shacks.

Marni   New Bocas Home

How about the weather?

Bocas del Toro has two seasons: wet and wetter. It receives an average of 115 inches of rainfall a year. While most of that falls from April to December, it's a significant amount of precipitation. The rain here is not like the monsoons of Southeast Asia where it can rain night and day for weeks. Days generally offer some sun and brief showers of heavy, intermittent rain. Beginning in January, rainfall is less, and picks up intensity in April.

Real estate prices in Bocas have skyrocketed and they'll probably continue to do so. A rundown, ramshackle house on the beach will cost much more than $50,000. You probably wouldn't live in it without extensive renovation. It might even be a total 'tear-down.'

Although Bocas appears ready for a boom, there are immediate problems with its infrastructure. Potable water, sewage treatment, and waste collection are all problems that must be dealt with, as they are marginally adequate today.

Some islands are privately owned and will operate exclusive resorts or retirement communities. Isla Solarte will be a planned retirement community. It is tranquil and surrounded by crystal blue water. This project is owned & is being developed by Americans. At the time of this writing, it is

still in the planning stage. Contact them at
www.tropicalproperties.com

Bocas is a wonderful vacation spot. It's
a little like Key West 100 years ago (or so
I'm told). Most people come as tourists to
snorkel, dive, surf, and lie in the sun on
snowy white beaches. Or snooze in a
hammock strung between two palm trees.

It's a midwinter's dream for those who
live in the frozen north, and who wish to
prove the highest and best use of the
pineapple is a frosty, *Pina Colada.*

But look it over carefully before
deciding to settle in here. Remember, it's
only a short flight from Panama City and
David. You can be on the beach of your
choice in a very short time.

• San Blas Islands

The Comarca de San Blas is the home
of the Kuna Indians, and has been granted a
form of sovereignty by the Panamanian
government. The Kunas are fiercely
independent and dedicated to maintaining
and saving their old ways and customs.

For example, a Kuna woman is not even
given a name until she has had her first

136

menstrual period. Until that day arrives, the young girl responds to a nick-name. The women dress traditionally, and wear a gold ring through their nose.

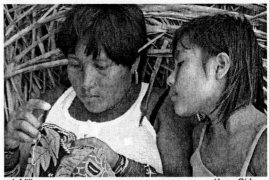

J. Miller   Kuna Girls

There is no possibility of buying property or retiring among the Kunas. However, the San Blas Islands are a fascinating and beautiful place to visit.

• Contadora Island – Pacific Coast

Long a favorite of Panamanians and Latin Americans, Contadora is in the Bay of Panama. It is only a fifteen- minute flight or one-hour boat ride from Panama City.

Contadora is not one of the larger of the Pearl Islands, but is considered Panama's most exclusive address. In Spanish, 'Contadora' means counting house.

In the 16th century, slaves were brought in to dive for pearls and cultivate the land of the islands. Today, the pearl beds are not nearly so productive, but one of the largest pearls in the world, the 31-carat *Peregrina* was found here. It was the property of several of Europe's Royal Families. It now belongs to Elizabeth Taylor.

Pearling still is practiced and the two best islands for buying are *Isla Casaya & Isla Casayeta,* about 12 km from Contadora. *Salvetore Fishing* will arrange transportation.

The beaches in the *Archipelago de las Perlas* are mostly light tan in color, like most of the beaches of Pacific waters, whether in Central America or California. The water is mostly turquoise, loaded with tropical fish swimming among the reefs, and aqueous home to leatherneck and hawksbill turtles. A snorkeler's dream.

Contadora is quite beautiful with at least a dozen secluded beaches and coves. The tradewinds here are quite regular. I talked with a California couple who bought a lovely condominium here a year ago. Two bedrooms, two baths, maid's quarters, etc., ($137,000) and while not right on the beach, they have a full beach view from

their living room and balcony. They told
me they have yet to turn on the air-
conditioner because of the cool trade
breezes.

Panama's only official nude beach,
Playa de las Suecas (Swedish Women's
Beach) is on Contadora, around the corner
and to the south of the Contadora Resort.
There are 12 beaches on this small (1.2
square km) island, and they are mostly
unoccupied except during holidays. The
permanent population is something less
than 350 people.

- ## *Hotel Punta Galeón*

A very nice hotel of 48 rooms. (250-
4134) Pool, sauna, kid's pool, restaurants,
bars, etc. $96/$120 night. Excellent beach.

The most crowded beach generally is
the one in front of the *Hotel Contadora
Resort*, Playa Larga. This beach also
affords an excellent opportunity for spotting
marine life, particularly amberjacks, manta
rays and both kinds of sea turtles.
Snorkeling here is nothing short of
fantastic. Snorkeling trips and guides can
be arranged at the hotel.

The Hotel Contadora Resort (507-250-4033) is large, with 354 rooms. Facilities include a huge pool, tennis courts, nine hole golf course, (all of which are free to guests) including mountain bikes, tennis rackets, and snorkeling equipment. Rates are about $80 (per person) per night, but these are open to negotiation as many guests arrive on package deals. All meals are included – buffet style.

Contadora has long been the near-exclusive playground of the wealthy. Many famous artists, writers, politicians, and executives from the world over have counted Contadora as their retreat, including the late Shah of Iran.

All of this plus the other accoutrements of the tropics: coral reefs, palm trees, sea turtles, parrots, and riots of tropical flora. There's one big difference here. You won't find raucous bars, wet tee-shirt contests, or a zillion students on Spring break.

There is a nine-hole golf course, two lovely (and quiet) resorts, a few shops, a new medical center, and several good restaurants. And, of course, the airstrip for the flight to Panama City.

The island is small, supply is small, so properties tend to be quite dear. Beachfront houses begin about $400,000 and up, depending on size. Properties off the beach are more reasonable: from a ball-park of $90,000 and up.

Then there's the lovely condominium units, mentioned earlier, under $200,000.

• Isla San Jose

The lovely resort of Hacienda del Mar was developed by the president of Aeroperlas, Panama's commuter airline. This is truly an upscale resort of 12 luxurious cabins, with a fine restaurant. The nightly rate is $250 per cabin, with a few larger cabins available.

Isla San Jose is a good-sized island of approximately 44 square km. An excellent road system was installed by the U.S. Navy several years ago. The island has 37 beaches, nine year round rivers, and several waterfalls. The Hacienda del Mar is the only development, so each cabin could have three private beaches. Talk about a honeymoon heaven!

The resort arranges tours, deep sea fishing expeditions, and four-wheeler explorations of the rainforest with its myriads of birds, flora and other fauna.

• Islas Tabogas

This group of small and close islands is in the Bay of Panama. Isla Tobaga is less than 600 hectares in size – about 1400 acres. It has a stormy history of pirates, murder, and sea battles.

Today, the only assaults on the island are weekending Panamanians who come to enjoy the resorts and beaches.

There is a ferry, the Calypso Queen, which leaves from Muelle 18 in the Balboa District of Panama City. The round trip fare is $7.50.

The day's entrance fee is $5.00 and entitles visitors to their free run of all beaches. The Hotel Tobaga rents umbrellas, paddle boats, hammocks, mats, and snorkeling equipment – all at reasonable prices.

There are no autos on the island, and besides the hotel there is only one other restaurant-bar, the Bar El Galeon. Nightlife is limited.

There is no property for sale here, but it's a fun and an inexpensive day's outing. Tobaga is a favorite of Panamanians.

Pacific Beaches

Approximately one hour from Panama City, miles of beaches begin. The coastline here is quite beautiful, and many investors (from many countries) and retirees are beginning to locate and/or invest in the properties along this stretch.

First class resorts are available where you can spend some time while investigating the area. Playa Coronado is little more than a one-hour drive from Panama City on the four-lane Interamericana Highway.

The *Hotel Coronado* is wonderful, and one of the best resorts in Panama. The *jardines* (gardens) are lovely, the staff is friendly, there's an Olympic size pool, Jacuzzi, tennis, equestrian center, spa, gym, and an excellent golf course designed by George Fazio. Restaurants are 1st class. Beaches are terrific.

Rooms are spacious with separate living and sleeping areas. About $175/night from

Dec-March, less later in season.
www.coronadoresort.com

This Beach area has grown in popularity over the years. Property prices are at a premium anywhere in the Coronado area, but if you shop, you can still find beach-front for less than $100,000.

Further west (about 25 km) is the huge resort of *The Royal Decameron*. This is probably the Pacific Coast's most popular resort with more than 600 rooms, pools, restaurants, spa, gym, tennis, discos, casino, beach and poolside bars, etc. One of the reasons it is so popular is its "all-inclusive" price. Less than $95 per person per day includes room, all meals, drinks (yes, drinks are included), equipment and access to everything. Friends of mine recently stayed here mid-week for $56 night. Reservations: 507-899-2111
www.decameron.com

Vista Mar

Only 55 miles west of Panama City is the new development of Vista Mar. This is a beautiful, gated community project that sits on terraced bluffs above the Pacific. Directions and signage are very clear from the Interamerican highway. This is a multi-layered project of more than 500 acres.

Multi-layered, by definition includes several choices available from raw lots, to condominiums, and single-family homes.

The condominiums are located in two towers of fourteen units each. The condominiums are a minimum of 858 square feet at $113,000 and go up to 2,255 square feet at $249,000.

The vacant lots for custom homes are located on the first terrace and are a minimum of ¼ acre – each with beautiful Pacific views.

There are clustered villas of 12 to 14 homes across the street from the golf course. These start at $129,500 for approximately 2,000 square feet up to $149,500 for 2,450 square feet. These clustered units each share a common area with a pool, social area, and children's park.

The homes on terraces 3-6 start at $255,000 (2816 square feet) up to 3,767 square feet at $296,000.

The golf course is scheduled for completion early 2006.

Each home or condo has an ocean view. The homes range in size starting at 1,800 square feet, with three bedrooms, two baths ($149,500) and up. Each home includes fully contained maid quarters with bath. The home designs generally place these quarters near the laundry room.

The project will have an 18-hole golf course, club-house, restaurant, and 50-room hotel. The architecture is dramatic.

Amenities include tennis, pools, health center, spa, bicycle paths, and an ecological park. Satellite TV and high speed internet connections are available for all units.

The development is only five minutes from El Rey Supermercado, bank, hardware store, beauty salon – even a veterinarian.

Whether you're retiring or looking for a second home, don't miss this spectacular development. For more details, contact them at: information@vistamarresort.com, Their website: www.vistamarresort.com

The Highlands

Not too far from Coronado Beach (19 km) is the new project of *Altos del Maria*. This is a major development by *The Grupo Melo, S.A.* The Melo Group is a very large company. They are the largest chicken and egg provider in Panama. Their eggs are in every store. They are also partners with Tyson for distribution in all of the Caribbean. Melo also owns the Izusu and John Deere distributorships in Panama, as well as the *Pio Pio* restaurants. They're well-funded, and the project shows it.

Altos del Maria is only 65 miles from Panama City, so it is easily accessed on the 4-lane, Interamerica highway. Its location is in the province of Panama, district of Chame.

I called the Sales Manager, Pedro Sarasqueta in Panama City on a Saturday morning. Since he was going out to the project, he insisted on driving me to the development.

It was quite warm in the coastal area, but we climbed on an excellent road to the property and were enjoying the cool fresh air of the highlands in a few minutes. The temperature at the entrance gate to *Los*

Altos del Maria was almost twenty degrees cooler than at the beach. Air conditioning definitely was not required.

The average year-round high temperature here is 68-degrees Fahrenheit. (20-degrees C) The average minimum is 61-degrees (F), 16-deg C, so the temperature is very uniform.

The landscape is lush, tropical greenery, and it's the habitat of hundreds of species of exotic birds, deer, and other small mammals. From the highest point on the project is a view of both the Atlantic and Pacific Oceans. Other views at lower elevations are almost as spectacular, but limited to either a Pacific Ocean view or of the lush valleys.

There are 350 lots in the current phase. Melo owns over 3,900 acres in these cool highlands. All roads are in (more than 27 miles of paved asphalt) with power and water to each lot.

Water is supplied from three aqueducts managed by the developer. The water source is the numerous, high quality year-round streams whose purity is exceptional.

Choose Panama . . .

Hutchings   Highlands View

Many lots have ocean views, and all are really well laid out. The engineering appears to be first-class and very much up to American standards.

The development takes advantage of the terrain, and rather than one large tract, there are several smaller units, each with a natural terrain separation. There are rivers, streams, waterfalls, wild orchids, and lovely scenery in this development.

Lot sizes range from about one-quarter acre to three-quarter's acre. Prices range from $18,000 to $40,000. Financing is available, and discounts apply for cash payment or the purchase of more than one lot.

Hutchings   Highlands Stream

Grupo Melo is <u>not</u> constructing homes. They are only selling the completed lots, but they can recommend several local contractors in the area, most of whom are quoting $35-$40 per square foot for construction. In observation of other building projects is Panama, this may be a low-ball price.

Telephone, high-speed internet, and satellite TV facilities are all available. An English speaking doctor is building a new medical clinic for the convenience of the residents. There is also a heliport on the project in the event an emergency or health evacuation is needed.

If you are thinking of buying property or building in Panama, you should definitely look at this project. There is no village yet, but a convenience market is

underway. The project is close to Panama City, close to the beach, Coronado Resort, Supermarkets, Golf, etc., yet has the fresh, cool air of the central highlands. Tel: (507) 260-4813
www.altosdelmaria.com

- ## El Valle Anton

Somewhat farther to the west is the charming community of El Valle Anton, known to the locals as simply 'El Valle.' This small community (6,500 pop) is nested in the crater of an extinct volcano. Its eruption three million years ago created one of the largest craters in all of the Americas – nearly 5 kilometers in diameter. The crater filled with rainwater over the eons, but between 25,000 and 10,000 BC, the lake drained, leaving a deep floor of sedimentation.

As the area became populated with humans, they settled here and began growing crops in the rich volcanic soil. Their arrival date is not factually determined, but the best estimate of most archeologists is approximately 10,000 to 15,000 years ago.

Because of its proximity to Panama City (about 75 miles) and its cool weather (about 2,000 feet in altitude), El Valle has been a long-time favorite of Panamanians wanting to get away from the tropical weather.

It has also become a favorite because of its Sunday market. A large handicrafts market where indigenous people bring their wares has become a tradition. Woven baskets from the Guyami, and even the finely woven treasures from the Wounaans as far away as Darien province are sold here. Panama hats from Ocú and Penemone are also sold, as well as fruit, vegetables, wood carvings, figurines, and pottery. Most items are less than $20. It's quite an affair.

Property here is less expensive than on the beaches or even further west in Boquete. If you believe, as I do, that a certain amount of expatriate community and activity is important, then you may want to think twice about settling in El Valle – lovely as it is. There are no new developments currently taking place, so your choices are pretty much limited to the existing homes.

On the other hand, if you would like to come to Panama and start a nice little bed and breakfast, El Valle might be a candidate. However, to be successful in the 'B & B' business, one needs a steady flow of potential customers. El Valle seems to have that on the weekends, but during the week, it can be 'iffy.'

El Valle is a very quiet little community with limited facilities, including medical. There are a number of smaller hotels and restaurants.

- *Hotel Don Pepe (507-983-6425)* $35-45 per night. 12 large rooms, clean, with private baths, & hot water. Communal TV and laundry. There is a good restaurant on the first floor offering several chicken and seafood dishes.

- *Hotel Rincon Vallero* (507-983-6175) 14 A-C rooms, private hot-water baths $65-95. Very good restaurant with shrimp, seafood, and steak specialties.

- *Hotel y Restaurante Los Capitanes* (507-983-6080) This is a nice place. Rooms are well-furnished with TV, VCRs and hotwater baths. Four rooms are outfitted for handicapped. Excellent restaurant and bar. $40-$80.

- ***La Casa de Lourdes (507-983-6450)*** An
  elegant hotel and restaurant in a Tuscan
  Villa style. Two rooms, surrounded by
  gardens and a pool. The excellent
  restaurant includes, meat, chicken, and
  seafood entrees.

  Again, we have not attempted to list all
  of the places to stay and eat. There are
  more facilities available in both categories.
  If you visit El Valle and these places are
  full, look around.

  Perhaps the greatest charm of El Valle
  lies in the fact it offers great walking trails
  for naturalists and birders.

  There is also a Canopy Adventure ride
  for the more daring. This is a suspended
  cable built within the tree canopy dozens of
  meters above the jungle floor. There are six
  platforms, and the ride takes you to all six.
  At one point, the ride will allow you to pass
  and look <u>down</u> at the 250-foot high Chorro
  El Macho (The Manly Waterfall). This ride
  requires personal strength and daring. It's
  not for everyone.

  El Valle also has a Museum and Zoo,
  and neither offers a lot for the visitor. Zoos
  in most Latin countries can be unkempt, sad

places. The Zoo at El Valle offers no surprise to either feature.

The Museo offers little to get excited about. There are some old petroglyphs of an earlier civilization, several religious artifacts, and information about the giant volcanic eruption that created the crater where El Valle currently sits.

The Western Highlands

Gateway to the western highlands is *David (Dah'veed)*, about 265 miles west of Panama City. This is the third largest city in Panama (130,000) and is the provincial capital. David is hot most of the time. And humid.

Primarily an agricultural center, David doesn't offer a lot of excitement as a place to settle in. However, David has many attractions. It is a first-rate supply center for automobiles, furniture, appliances, and hardware.

Chiriqui Province is the breadbasket of Panama. More fruit, vegetables, and cattle are raised here than in all of Panama. And

the coffee plantations in the Chiriqui
Highlands are wonderful to see and tour.

One of the best supermarkets in Panama
is Super Baru located in eastern David.
There is also *PriceSmarts*, an affiliate of
Costco. They honor the Costco card, and
have many of the products you'll find in
Costco stores the world over.

David also has a number of good shops,
two major hospitals, and a third under
construction. As the provincial capital,
there are many attorneys, notary publics,
banks, travel agencies, an immigration
office, doctors, dentists, and other
professionals.

David is a major transportation hub.
Buses to Panama City, Costa Rica, Volcan,
and Boquete originate in the central bus
terminal.

Express Buses to Panama City offer
comfortable seats, and movies for about
$15 (one way). The trip supposedly takes
six hours, but with construction repairs to
the Interamerican Highway, allow seven.

David has an excellent airport with at
least three flights daily to Panama City and
Bocas del Toro. There is no bus service

from the airport to town, but taxis are
plentiful and cheap (About $2).

David is also home to one of the best
deep-sea sport fishers in Panama, *Pesca
Panama.* (507-614-5850) This firm
operates off of Coiba Island, Hannibal
Bank, which is one of the world's great
fisheries and near David. Many world
records have originated here.

There are several good places to stay in
David.

- *Hotel Gran Nacional* (507-
  775-2222) In central David. A
  modern hotel with good
  restaurant, pizzeria, large pool,
  casino, and parking. All rooms
  have 50-chan. TV, AC, & Hot
  water. Four theatres are located
  across the street. $45-$60.
  Probably the best hotel in town.

- *Hotel Castilla* (507-)774-5260
  Centrally located. All rooms
  have AC, Hot water, Cable TV.
  Good value at $25-30.

- *Hotel Puerta del Sol* - Rooms
  about $27. Fair restaurant, Bar,
  TV, A/C. My objection to this

place is its lack of security.
Door locks are the bedroom,
push-button type. I never had a
problem here with theft of any
kind, but it was always a worry
to leave the room.

Each March, David hosts a large,
international fair (Feria de San Jose de
David). Every type of merchandise under
the sun, from automobiles to home
furnishings, is available. The fair is
immensely popular. The horse show and
rodeo are important features.

- Transportation: The bus
  terminal is on Avenida del
  Estudiante. It is crowded, and
  buses leave regularly to many
  cities and towns. If you're
  going to *Volcan*, the bus leaves
  every hour from 5AM to 5PM.
  The trip takes about 1-1/2 hours
  and the fare is $2.30

  The buses leave for *Boquete*
  every 25-minutes. It takes about
  45-minutes and the fare is $1.20.

  Express buses to *Panama City*
  10AM, 2PM, 10PM, and

midnight take about six or seven
hours ($15) and terminate at the
Albrook terminal.

Tracopa (775-0585) provides
bus service to San Jose, Costa
Rica, departing daily at 8:30
AM from the Trapoca office at
Avenida 5 Este and Calle A Sur.
The trip takes about 8 hours and
the fare is $12.50.

Beaches Near David

- *Las Olas Resort* (507-772-3000)
  This is a large new complex.
  Facilities include a bar-
  discotheque, restaurant, gym,
  beauty salon and spa. Room
  rates are about $85. Beach front
  lots were offered for $35,000,
  and I'm told were quickly
  gobbled up. More coming.

- *Playa Las Lajas* is 62 km (36
  miles) east of David. Light sand
  and palms line this portion of
  the coast. Lodging and
  restaurant facilities are limited.

The Western Highlands

- *Volcan*

This village lies to the west of David, is an agricultural community, as is most of this area, and perched on the northwestern slopes of Volcan Baru. At 11,400 feet high, this dormant volcano is the highest mountain is Panama.

The province of Chiriqui shares its border with Costa Rica, and Volcan is approximately 10-miles due east at an altitude of nearly 5,000 feet. It may be quite a good place to retire. The weather is moderate (about 68-75 degrees F the year round.) The population is nearing 7,000 (in the surrounding area) with an expatriate community of 60 families – and growing

In addition to markets and shops, there is a medical clinic in Volcan, and the nearby towns of Bambito and Cerro Punta are also delightful. Bambito is the home of the 4-star *Hotel Bambito* with its tennis courts, pool, hot tub and sauna, horseback riding, etc. Rates are a little pricey, ranging from $120-145, but it's a lovely retreat.

There are ruins of a pre-Columbian culture in nearby ***Barriles***. These ruins are on private land, so don't go traipsing across the fields without getting permission from the owner.

There's an American expatriate living in Volcan, Bill Hemmingway (507-284-4175, or 507-232-5443 evenings) who will be happy to tell you of the many advantages about retiring in Volcan. Bill arranges nature hikes, bird-watching tours, and trips through the national park and rain forest, as well as scenic drives to Costa Rica or across the continental divide to the Caribbean. He can guide you to property and brokers.

Real Estate prices in and around Volcan are substantially less than those in Boquete. A hectare of land (2.47 acres) in or near town can be purchased for $0.80 per square meter (about $3,500/acre)

Interesting places nearby are Cerro Punta, Lagunas de Volcan (Lakes of Volcan), and Guadalupe. The *Sendero Los Quetzals* is a famous trail through the forest which will take you all the way back to Boquete. Many people hire a guide and drive to Cerro Punta, then walk downhill to Boquete. Your chances of seeing the Resplendent Quetzal on this hike are excellent.

Los Quetzales Lodge and Spa (507-771-2182) is a 10-room lodge with restaurant and bars, with a lovely dining room. Rooms are $50-60. About 600 meters above the lodge is a beautiful orchid sanctuary, ***Finca Dracula.*** More than 2,000 species of orchids are grown here – one of Latin America's finest exhibitions. A modest fee of $7. is requested.

The Parque Internacional La Armistad is over one million acres in size and ranges across the Costa Rican border. This is a fabulous park. Most of the Panamanian portion of the park lies in the province of Bocas del Tore, but entrance is more accessible from Cerro Punta.

The plant and animal life in this park represent the most diverse in the entire country. If you're a birding fanatic, the park is sensational. In addition, there are several varieties of felines who make the park their habitat, including jaguars, ocelots, and margays.

In retrospect, the area west of David offers great potential for retirement. Property is more than reasonable, it's close to David, the climate is great, and there are a number of expatriate families living here.

Eastern Highlands

Boquete

- Boquete leads the pack when it comes to charm. Of course, that's not all.

- It leads the pack in the number of expatriates who reside here – most of them full-time.

- It leads the pack in new housing and land developments.

- It probably leads the pack in land prices – but they're still a fraction of what you'd pay in the States, Canada, or Europe. (Please be cautious about buying property on a whim) See ***Business Opportunities.***

I arrived in Boquete (Bo-ket-āy) after spending several days in Panama City, where the temperature was warm but not as oppressively hot as I anticipated. Panama City was a bustling, vibrant, urban metropolis. It was great. The sights, the history, the shopping, the canal, the hotels, and the restaurants will bring me back again.

I didn't know what to expect in Boquete, except I knew it was a small village nestled in a lush green valley. Rather than take the $1.20 bus, I took a taxi. I was lugging a large duffle bag, a carry-on bag for essentials (in case the airlines sent my duffle to Tierra del Fuego), and my lap-top computer.

The taxi from David airport to Boquete was $15. I couldn't help but compare that to the $44 shuttle fare between Newport Beach and LAX. About the same distance.

Of course the shuttle driver spoke a little more English than my taxi driver, but he really didn't have much to say that I wanted to hear. The fare comparison was just the beginning of the many comparisons I was to make in the next three weeks.

After settling in at ***The Petite Hotel Mozart***, I wanted to see Boquete.

Hutchings   Mozart Terrace

Hutchings   Breakfast Terrace   Mozart Hotel

I called a taxi that took me into the village – about a six-minute ride. The fare was $1.25 — and while I'm at it, the taxi drivers here are sane, unlike those in Panama City, whose object in life seems to be to come as close to another vehicle as possible without inflicting major damage.

However, a word here about the Panama drivers: their taxis appear to be generally undamaged – not like the wrecks seen in Mexico City.

My first stop was at ***Boquete Highlands Realty*** where I met Kelly Collier, a real estate broker who had lived in Hawaii before putting his roots down in Boquete.

Kelly was gracious and informative. He thought the climate in Boquete was superior to Hawaii. Not as hot or as rainy, although it showers every afternoon from May to October, and rains hardest in November.

He told me small furnished rental homes would run about $350-400/month. Unfurnished $250-350. (Yankee dollars)

Basic lot prices for ¼ to ½ acre were running about $20,000 to $35,000 depending on view, etc.

New home construction would run about $45-$50 square ft. No one had heating or air conditioning, except a few gringos were putting in fireplaces.

A small *finca* or coffee farm would be priced in the range of $50,000 to $75,000 per *hectare* (2.47 acres)

Obviously, these were generalized prices and could vary in value by view, micro-climate, availability of water, phones, and power. I was to discover more about pricing.

Kelly was kind enough to take me out to a new development, *Valle Escondido (Hidden Valley)*. My jaw dropped when I first saw this project. This is a guarded-gate community, with golf course, riding stables, a small village, an ampitheatre, and a cantina – it looked like an exclusive development in Southern California or Florida. It was immaculate.

Construction is stucco with red-tiled roofs and the architecture right out of Tuscany.

I met the developer, Sam Taliaferro of Valle Escondido. The project was multi-layered, with duplexes, single-family residences, and building lots for sale. It is a gorgeous community. Prices start at $162,000 for a 2-bedroom, 2-bath duplex. Financing is available. At the time of my visit, they were nearly sold out.

A new section of 2-bedroom, 2-bath condominiums will be open soon. The prices are projected to be about $150,000.

Hutchings   Valle Escondido Duplex   Boquete

A spa, swimming pool, Jacuzzi, exercise facility, and a holistic health center will be open by December 2005.

Mr. Taliaferro's concept has been to bring an upscale development to Boquete. His background has been in the high tech industry where he holds several patents. Naturally, high speed internet connections are in place as well as underground utilities.

Valle Escondido is a first-class development. Mr. Taliaferro also owns a restaurant in Boquete as well as a very fine hotel, *Los Establos*.

After leaving *Valle Escondido*, I went downtown (less than two minutes) to locate Pan-Am Construction Company.

Pan-Am specializes in custom-built homes in the Boquete area. They build turn-key homes, including all appliances. They take pride in their engineering, construction, design, and craftsmanship.

The choice of woods available in Panama is mind-boggling. There is no such thing as particle board or veneers. All cabinetry is Teak, Coco-Bolo, or other local hardwoods. These woods were some of the most beautiful I've ever seen. A wide range of finishes is available.

Same choices on doors. No hollow core doors here. They're all beautiful, solid panel doors – made locally, in Boquete.

Plumbing fixtures are American Standard. Appliances, generally Whirlpool, included large refrigerator, gas range, washer and dryer. Flooring is glazed Italian tile. Roofs are tile, and the entire house is seismically structured. Average cost: $50 square foot.

Bob Waterstripe, owner of Pan-Am, told me that people coming to Boquete were generally downsizing from their homes in the States. The most popular plans seemed to be in the 1500 sq ft range. The smaller homes have 2 bedrooms, 2 baths, with lots of glass and outdoor living under roof.

Choose Panama . . .

Pan-Am maintains a staff of architects and designers to customize the homes, and several people have committed for much larger residences.

Bob Waterstripe is knowledgeable and very personable. He takes great pride in building a quality product. His door is open to work directly with all prospects without intermediaries.

Pan-Am recently developed Alta Vista, a project of 14 lots, averaging more than ¼ acre. The development has wide streets and an on-site lake. All other utilities are installed. Many lots have views. Prices ranged from $19,000 to $39,900 and the Alta Vista project sold out quickly.

Pan-Am is putting the final touches on another new project. There will be about 65 lots, which will be generally larger than those in Alta Vista, and most will have ocean views. Prices had not been established at the time of this writing, but Pan-Am's projection was they would be in the $30,000 range. Pan-Am maintains their offices in the Global Bank building on Avenida Central. (507) 720-1775

There are other builders in the area, and I've interviewed several expatriates who have bought existing homes and remodeled or built new homes. Some are making the remodeling business an avocation.

With building costs at less than $50 per square foot, it's easy to see how one can build a 1,000 square foot home on a $25,000 lot and have a home for less than $80,000.

A word of caution: Boquete is becoming popular, and as such, may attract a variety of real estate 'operators.'

Again, exercise caution when thinking of a raw property purchase. Hire an attorney. Before making an offer, insist on 'comparables,' and don't be rushed into an offer by the 'scare' tactics some salespeople may employ.

A local real estate attorney in Boquete is Sra.Victoria Romero (507) 720-1086. "Vickie" is the wife of the local doctor, Leonidas Pretelt, and a very reputable member of the community. She specializes in rental and "for sale" property in the Boquete area. She is very knowledgeable.

Another attorney is Lea del R. Adames Francheschi. Her offices are in David (507) 774-4426. Sra. Adames is a full-service attorney, and an expert in Panamanian real estate and labor laws.

New Projects

Two new developments are planned near Boquete. Each of which is being directed to different focused markets.

Cielo Paraiso is a beautiful, exclusive planned community near Boquete with a championship 18-hole golf course - to be constructed in 2005.

Raideep and Colleen Lal arrived in Boquete from Toronto, Canada. They've been in Boquete two years, looking for the ultimate in lifestyle and climate. And they brought their dream with them – to develop a luxury, golf course community at affordable prices.

They bought the property for *Cielo Paraiso* after commissioning one of the world's foremost golf course architects, Michael Poellot. Mr. Poellot has designed more than 300 courses the world over – Europe, Canada, the U.S., Southeast Asia,

South Africa, and Japan boast some of his more well-known courses.

To supplement the 160 exclusive building sites surrounding the course (most lots are in the ½ to ¾ acre size), the Lals hired The Warren Group from Santa Barbara, California to design a hotel and clubhouse. These exclusive facilities include the only convention facilities in the Western Highlands. They are the ultimate in luxury, and will include every amenity imaginable, from tennis courts, spa, restaurants, pool, etc.

Construction will begin in late 2004, although some earth moving has already begun.

Hacienda Los Molinos is another development being marketed by Raideep and Colleen Lal. This is another upscale project just south of Boquete,. Their slogan is *"Hay lugares que te quitan el aliento."* A literal interpretation is: ***"There are places that take your breath away."*** *Truly.*

This planned community will have homes ranging from 1,650 square feet to more than 3,000 square feet. The amenities are superb – including club house, pool,

Jacuzzi, tennis courts, arts & crafts studio,
wood shop, exercise room, restaurant, bar,
and library/lounge.

In addition, the community has been
designed with retirees specifically in mind.
A care facility (a full-time nurse will be
employed), with massage, health services,
and physiotherapy facilities. Activities will
include crafts, cooking lessons, dancing,
and nightly movies.

This is an ambitious project and has
been beautifully thought out and designed.
There are only 82 lots available. Lots and
homes are anticipated to begin at $150,000.
Of course, the larger homes will be
commensurately more. Custom lots will be
available from the mid-twenties. The Lals
have arranged 50% financing on lots and
homes. (507) 720-2431

Colleen Lal can be contacted at :
colleen@boqueterealestate.com

Exploring Boquete

Boquete sits in a small bowl of a valley
at the eastern base of Volcan Baru, at an
altitude of 3,200 feet. The altitude accounts
for its spring-like weather the year round.

The village has good shopping. There are two large markets with a good selection of meat, produce, and most commodities imaginable. Of course, many people make the 22 mile trek to David on occasion to stock up at *Super Baru* or *Price Smarts,* but the local markets do a nice job.

There are clothing stores, an electronics store, a computer store, bakeries, pharmacies, etc. Gift stores galore. There's also a public market with some of the best produce you'll ever crunch into. It's really inexpensive, and really fun to attend. Locals, expatriates, and the Ngobe-Guaymi Indians come to the village every Saturday.

Boquete Climate

One of the biggest attractions to Boquete is its climate. The temperature is constant – a spring-like 75 degrees (F) almost every day of the year. However, the nights are cool – averaging 60 degrees (F). Cool enough to require sleeping under a light blanket at night. You'll also need a jacket or sweatshirt in the evenings.

The rainy season starts in May and lasts through November. A typical day during the rainy season is sunny until noon or one o'clock. Then, clouds will gather and one or two showers can be expected in the afternoon or evening – punctuated by sunshine.

Showers can be intense, and as November approaches, can become quite heavy. But it's still pleasant.

Of course, it does rain once in a while in the 'dry' season, but infrequently. Just enough to maintain the wonderful greenery that surrounds Boquete.

How about the humidity? Boquete is almost 3,500 feet in altitude, and humidity hardly exists. Certainly nothing like the coastal areas, and not even close to the muggy, clinging humidity of Washington, DC, St. Louis, or Miami.

How About Bugs?

Panama has established a reputation for harboring mosquitoes. And, it's well-deserved if you're on the coast or in the coastal jungles where mangrove swamps and still water offer a perfect breeding environment.

I stayed in Boquete for almost three months and saw very few mosquitoes.

Certainly not enough to even consider them as a pest. A true testimonial to this is the Palo Alto Restaurant whose dining room is roofed, but otherwise completely open.

Guides

One of the best things to do when arriving in a new town is to look for a guide. If you don't speak Spanish, then find a guide who speaks English.

There are several excellent guides in Boquete. There are those who concentrate on touring the coffee farms and processing facilities. **Terry and Hans van der Vooren** are acknowledged experts in the world of coffee, and they also specialize in birding and nature tours (507-720-3852).

Boquete Mountain Cruisers is operated by **Patsy Underhill**. Ms Underhill has a wealth of knowledge and experience in the travel business. She has been a resident of Boquete for several years. (507) 720-4697 or 624-0350.

Richard Livingston is an American who offers his Guide Services, which are very complete, at very reasonable rates. (507) 636-9887

Boquete is world renowned for its coffee, perhaps the finest in the world. The valley is small, and the environment is ideal – rich, volcanic soil, cool weather, and coffee farmers who have worked for generations developing the finest Arabic trees possible. There are a number of processors in the area and tours of their facilities are also available. If you love coffee, you'll be enchanted with Boquete.

Birding Around Boquete

Birding is exciting in this small valley. The resplendent Quetzal is here, among hundreds of other species. The door was open to my room the other day and a beautiful, small *"perrico"* flew in for a short visit. He was a gorgeous blue-green-yellow specimen. His visit was short, and he flew out as fast as he flew in. Maybe he determined I didn't have any bananas.

If you do go off into the jungle, don't do it without a guide. Some friends just came back from a hike down the Quetzal Trail (about 8 hours). It had rained all day. When the group reached the bottom of the trail where their pick-up ride was supposed to be, the bridge had washed out.

The *Rio Caldera* was raging, and it was impossible to cross. Their guide went upstream a ways and found where local Indians had felled two large trees across a narrow part of the river. The entire group nervously scrambled across the tree falls, holding on for dear life, because if someone had fallen in the torrent, it would have meant serious injury or drowning. All's well that ends well, but they had quite an adventure, and it's fortunate no one was hurt.

Living Costs - Boquete

- Living costs are substantially lower than in the U.S.

- *Direct TV* (satellite) is less than $50 month and includes many stations from the U.S.

- Telephones: Land lines basically are about $20.

- An *ADSL* Internet connection is an additional $35.

- International calling (to the U.S.) with Dial-Pad runs $0.037 per minute.

- Cell phones are in wide use and service is excellent. (I bought one for $39 and used it for three months – phone cards ($10) are used to pay for the calls.

- Electricity: about $25 per month

From local markets:

Filet Mignon	$3.00 lb
Prime Ground Sirloin	$1.65 lb
92% Lean Ground Beef	$0.65 lb
Pork Tenderloin	$1.90 lb
Eggs XL - Brown	$0.45 doz
Fresh Bread (Bakery)	$0.35 loaf
Fresh Butter	$2.00 lb
Milk (Homo)	$0.90 qt
Local Coffee	$2.10 lb

I just enjoyed the world's very best tomato. This tomato was even better than the ones my grandfather

raised in his home garden. It cost
$0.11 at Romero's Mercado.

Prices may be lower at *Super
Baru* in David and the selection is
greater. *Price Smarts* also has good
values, but like any Costco store,
you must buy in larger quantities.

Fresh seafood and fish are
comparably lower – the Pacific is
only 22 miles from Boquete.
Vegetables are inexpensive and
wonderful – they are raised locally,
and organic vegetables are
abundant. Fresh Rainbow trout are
raised here in the cool streams.

Even though the valley is small, there
are several micro-climates in and around
Boquete. As you climb out of Boquete to
the north and west, you can find yourself in
the cloud-forest within three miles. At
some time during the day (more prevalent
in early morning and late afternoon) you
will encounter a very fine, floating mist. It
is called *The Bajareque (Baha-raykay).*

When water droplets are refracted in the
sunlight, spectacular rainbows are formed,
known as the *Arco Iris*. Sometimes, you
will see multiple rainbows. It's quite a

sight. But this light mist is also one of the climatic features that makes Boquete such a wonderful growing environment for vegetables - and particularly coffee. In Viet Nam, a similar phenomenon is known as "rain dust."

Places to Stay - Boquete

As in Panama City, we won't give a complete listing of every hotel and hostel, but enough really good ones from which you can start your selection process. If you are visiting for a month or more, be sure to ask each hostelry if they have long-term rates.

Also, if you are going to be here a while, look into the availability of short-term house rentals.

Hotels

- *Hotel La Petite Mozart* (507-720-3764) Three rooms. $19/26; $35; and $45 for a suite. Turn left on Volcancito Road, as you come into Boquete. If you pass the large IPAT structure on the right, you've gone 50 yards too far. Turn left on Volcancito about two miles. This is

truly a petite and charming hotel
serving excellent meals and wine.

The proprietress is Lorenza
Diaz, artist, jewelry maker, and *chef
extraordinaire*. Located on 2
hectares of coffee farm, the view
from her breakfast terrace is lovely.
She speaks Spanish, English, and
German.

• *Hotel Panamonte* (507-720-
1327) At the north end of town
before crossing the *Rio Caldera*.
This is the *Grande Dama* of hotels
in Boquete. Built in the 1920's, it
has a lovely dining room, beautiful
gardens and a comfortable bar and
lounge – with fireplace. This hotel
is quite special. Even if you don't
stay here, having a cocktail or
dinner is an absolute must. Rooms
about $65.

• *Las Cabanas de la Via Lactea* (507-720-2376) Pilar and Flavio Nobili built this charming complex on a beautiful piece of property that backs up to the *Rio Caldera.* The 10 lodgings consist of five 2-story hexagonal buildings, strategically located in a garden-like setting. Rooms are large and comfortable with kitchen facilities and large baths. About $45/plus tax for two, commensurately more for larger units and more people. Long-term rates available. I stayed here for two months, and have never enjoyed nicer, more attentive hosts.

www.lavialactea.biz

• *Hotel Los Establos (507-720-2685)* Owned by Sam Taliaferro, developer of the

185

beautiful *Valle Escondido.* The hotel is every bit as nice as his premier development. The hotel sits high on a slope in the Palo Alto area looking down on the Boquete valley across pasture land, coffee fincas, and the village of Boquete. Elegant rooms from $165 to suites $235.

• *La Montana y el Valle – The Coffee Estate Inn* (507-720-2211) Three luxurious bungalows with complete kitchens, living/dining room and separate bedroom. This is a working coffee farm with trails leading into the forest. No children under 9. Barry Robbins and Jane Walker, Canadian Expatriates, prepare wonderful meals for guests only. Coffee is roasted daily. A bungalow price of about $90 includes brief tours.

Boquete Restaurants

Dining in Boquete ranges from *typico* Panamanian food to basic pizza parlors to *hamburgesas* to elegance. The pizza parlors are generally along Avenida Central.

Choose Panama . . .

Thankfully, the closest thing to "fast food" is the Java Juice restaurant for *hamburguesas and smoothies. (It's good.)*

- ***Bistro,*** a restaurant near the village center, is popular with the gringo community. The food is good. The mushroom soup ($2 bowl) is terrific. They have a complete bar and a good selection of wines. Dinners from $6.

- ***Panamonte*** is probably one of the nicer restaurants in all of Chiriqui province. Built in the 1920's, the *Panamonte* exemplifies Panama. The bar is exceptionally comfortable, and the food is very good. Dinners from $7.   White tablecloths, silver service, and flowers are on every table. The ceiling fans add to the tropical environment. The hotel has lovely gardens and an especially comfortable lounge with fireplace.

- ***Palo Alto*** is a unique, new restaurant that serves excellent food and has a lovely selection of wines. The restaurant is located just a couple of kilometers from central

Boquete on Palo Alto Road. It's dining room is open to the Rio Caldera - with the wildness of the jungle just on the opposite river bank. Try their *Beef Brochette* . Dinners from $7

- ***Restaurante La Huaca*** on Avenida Central. A nicely restored home serving excellent Italian food from really good pizzas to pasta. Full bar and excellent wines. A popular rendezvous for locals and expatriates. Dinners from $6

- ***The Santa Fe*** just across the bridge near the center of town – opposite the flower gardens. Nice menu, but famous for its hamburgers. They're huge and delicious. The Santa Fe is especially popular with its "Happy Hour" on Friday afternoons.

Stores & Shopping

Groceries

Two good markets: **Romero's** and **The Mandarin.** Each have a broad selection of products, both local and American. Each has quality dairy products, produce, and a good butcher shop. The Mandarin has

other items, i.e., clothing, etc. At the time
of this writing, Romero's was adding a deli
and bakery.

General Merchandise

There are many other stores in Boquete
ranging from Auto Supply, Computers,
Department Stores, Pharmacies, Gift Shops,
Hardware Stores, etc.   There are three
Bakeries in town, none of which is great.

Medical

Boquete and its citizens are fortunate to have
an imminently qualified physician/surgeon in
practice. Dr. Leonidas Pretelt, speaks excellent
English. His clinic is open Monday through
Saturday, and he is highly recommended in the
community. He even makes house calls!
David is only 22 miles away with major
medical facilities and hospitals.   Most people
seem to travel to David for dental care.

Spanish Lessons

There are two excellent instructors in Boquete.
Rebecca Hill owns the *Oasis Internet Café* and also
instructs small groups. Her rates are reasonable ($6
per lesson) and everyone seems to like the sessions and
profess to learn a lot.

Marie Boyd was a teacher in the Panama City school system for many years. She is married to Bob Boyd who grew up in the Canal Zone. Marie has instructed students of many corporate accounts, i.e., Sony, etc. She charges $6/hour and will come to your home for private lessons. Call 720-2539; or cell 606-3554 in Boquete.

Expatriate Community

Boquete has a large, and growing, community of expatriates from the world over. There are many from the United States and Canada, but also families from all of the Americas and Western Europe. The community is not only socially active, but holds regular meetings on many subjects that pertain to living in Boquete, including construction, gardening, materials, real estate law, etc. Everyone is welcome. *At the time of this writing, meetings were held weekly and were well-attended.*

Hutchings   Expat Gathering

Socially, the expatriates hold a monthly potluck – generally on a Sunday afternoon. I attended two events and had a wonderful experience each time. Incidentally, they were well-attended by several Panamanian residents. These afternoons were thoroughly enjoyable.

After meeting several expatriates, I thought their stories might be of interest. They've come from all walks of life and professions.

Most of them had a common desire, which became a thread linking them together: *They all wanted to live in a place that had a wonderful climate and where they could live within their means.*

Meet the Expatriates

Hershel & Mikey Stolebarger

When Hershel and Mikey Stolebarger retired, they bought a motor home. Hershel had been a real Estate broker in Albuquerque, NM for 27 years, and they wanted to see the country and search for a place where they might settle down at a reasonable cost. They traveled for two years, staying in campgrounds and sometimes functioning as campground hosts. Even when they were hosts, and the campground gave them free rent and electricity for their motor home, they had difficulty living within their retirement income.

They started searching for a more economical lifestyle and one where they could enjoy a nice climate and have a good standard of living on their retirement benefits. It didn't appear they could do so in the States, so they looked at Puerto Rico, Mexico, and Costa Rica as possibilities. One day, Hershel picked up some information on Panama via the Internet. Panama looked pretty good, and they decided to take a trip to investigate.

That was two and a half years ago. They liked what they saw in Panama and made the decision to move. They settled on Boquete because of its mild, spring-like weather year round. They felt comfortable having the U.S. dollar as the currency, and they could safely drink the water out of the tap.

After renting for a few months, they found a building site (about a third of an acre), and decided to build a modest home. They hired a Panamanian contractor and built a lovely small home of about 1,100 square feet. It has two bedrooms, two baths, a large kitchen, and a large living-dining area. The ceramic tile floors are beautiful and the hardwood cabinetry and doors could only be found in Panama. Their outdoor covered living space is over 500 square feet. Needless to say, with the Boquete weather, they utilize their outdoor living to its fullest.

I asked them what they liked most about Panama in general, and specifically, Boquete. "What's not to like?" Hershel said. "This is a place retirees like us could only dream about on our income." Mikey went on to expound about the expatriate community. "We've met some really lovely people and made many friends here."

Hutchings   Stolebarger House

"And we don't have to worry about an unstable monetary system in Panama. The U.S. dollar is the currency. We could open a local bank account, but we have our Social Security checks sent to a U.S. bank and just pull out what we need from the local ATM's."

Hershel and Mikey are active hikers and birders. They love to walk the highlands, and they not only grow their own coffee, they bought a small roaster and roast their own beans. They love to garden. They also grow their own citrus, and their flowers are beautiful.

Their view is spectacular and overlooks a lush green valley typical of the Panama highlands. The house was designed for outdoor living and they have about 500 square feet under roof surrounding the living and kitchen areas.

Their cost, house and lot: About $80,000. Because of the climate in Boquete, they don't need heating or air conditioning. And, the cost of living is economical. "We do a lot of barbequing," Mikey said. "Filet Mignon is about $3 a pound. And our maid is $1 an hour. We take Spanish lessons twice a week. They're $6 a lesson, and we're having a lot of fun."

How about Medical? "We have the local Medical Insurance, and the local doctor not only speaks English, he's an excellent physician."

I asked them about TV. They have *Direct Satellite* TV with many of their favorite programs from the States – in English. "And we have a fast internet service here," Hershel said. "It's ADSL."

Mikey smiled and said, "We have an international telephone service called *Dial Pad.* We have three children and five grandkids. We call our kids and family in the States for about four cents a minute. It's so easy to stay in touch. I love that."

Hershel and Mikey are living the good life within their retirement benefits. They found their place in Boquete, Panama.

Dave and Cora Kent

Dave and Cora Kent are hikers and climbers. They have always enjoyed taking vacations where they could pursue their love of nature and adventure, and have done so all over the world – the U.S., Canada, Europe, and Asia.

Cora enjoyed an active practice as a real estate attorney in St. Petersburg, Florida. Dave's career path had led him into being National Construction Manager for a well-known, fast food chain.

Hutchings   Cora Kent

Choose Panama . . .

In March of 2003, Dave and Cora visited Panama on a vacation to climb the 11,400 ft extinct volcano, Volcan Baru, the highest mountain in Panama. Retirement was the last thing on their minds. They arrived in Boquete, and used it as a base for their climb. While in town, they decided to look at houses. After all, real estate was their vocation and avocation, since they also bought older houses and renovated them for resale.

They looked at several smaller houses on the market. One, in particular, caught their eye. It was on a pleasant street, had a lovely outlook, and needed only a modest amount of work to bring it up to U.S. standards. It was also under $30,000. They liked it.

The next day, they started the climb up Mt. Baru with their guide. About three hours into the climb, they turned around to view the Boquete valley below. It was a beautiful sight, with the Pacific Ocean about thirty miles away, but in view. Cora looked at Dave. Their thoughts were identical. "Let's go buy that house," Cora said. Dave smiled. "My thoughts exactly." They never completed the climb.

They turned around, went down the trail, marched into the real estate office, and made a full price offer. It was accepted immediately. They flew back to Florida, Cora sold her law practice, and Dave wound up his personal affairs. They had traveled to Boquete to climb a mountain, not to retire.

They are really happy to be in Boquete. They made modest upgrades to the small home, did a little painting, some cabinet work, and added a verandah. I asked them if they have fully retired.

"Not really," Dave said. "We've just bought another house and we're going to fix it up a little, resell it, and maybe do it again."

They also enjoy working in the yard. "The flowers here are gorgeous," Cora said. "And the birds. My gosh, the birds. They're incredible."

Dave smiled. "The big yard stuff we leave to the gardener. He comes once a week and works all day, about ten hours. We just kind of putter around."

"How much does that cost," I asked.

Dave smiled again. "Ten Bucks a day."

Cora said, "But Rosa, the maid, is only six dollars a day. She comes twice a week, but doesn't put in so many hours."

"Was your family surprised about your decision to move?" Cora's eyes twinkled. "A little, but our daughter is coming for a visit next month. We're all looking forward to it."

"Do you miss the States?"

"This is a great place to be," Dave said. "If we get homesick, which so far we haven't, Miami is only 2-1/2 hours from Panama City. We're no farther from home than if we were in Chicago."

We were at the kitchen table and I looked up Mt. Baru, which filled the window frame in the distance. "How about the mountain?"

Cora looked at Dave. "Someday. But right now, we have Spanish lessons twice a week, we have our yard, we have the new house to fix up, we have our many expat friends here, and oh, yes, we do have a hiking group where we're going to try the Quetzal trail and look for that beautiful bird."

"Bird?" I asked.

"The resplendent Quetzal, the most beautiful bird in the world. It's here in Panama."

It's a nice feeling to interview happy people.

Dan & Jeannie Miller

Dan and I were having a beer in the Panamonte Hotel in Boquete. Jeannie had just flown back to the States on a family emergency.

The Panamonte is one of those places that seems to put us back a few years. A light rain had begun to fall outside our window. We were in the lounge area sitting in overstuffed chairs, and one of the staff was lighting a fire in the fireplace.

I asked Dan if he'd mind talking a little about Boquete. He said he'd be happy to answer a few questions.

"Dan, what was your career in the States?"

"In our working days, I was a private attorney in Washington, DC specializing in communications. I worked with the FCC getting licenses, etc. for my clients. Jeannie had been a flight attendant for a major international airline."

"Did you retire?"

"We retired and sailed the Caribbean in our 46-foot sloop. We'd been on the boat for seven years, and came to Boquete almost by accident. Bocas del Toro in Panama was one of our stops in the Caribbean. The weather was hot, wet, and humid. Some friends

200

suggested we take a break and go to Boquete. It's not very far from Bocas, distance-wise, but it's a world apart climatically and socially.. We liked it so much, we bought a building lot."

"Was that on a whim?"

"Jeannie and I had talked a lot about making a life-style change. We love the boat, but seven years non-stop and it was time for something else. We hadn't come to Boquete for that reason. We just wanted to get away from the heat and the bugs. As it turned out, we fell in love with this place."

"That was a big decision."

"In some ways, yes. But we still own the boat and can always go back to the sailing life."

"What do you like best about Panama?"

"Lots. The country is beautiful, and you have the diversity of a first world city down in Panama, miles of beaches, and a very lush countryside. The cost of living is low, and we don't have to worry about currency devaluations, etc. The climate is great, the Panamanians are nice people, and the expatriate community here is special."

"Do you worry about medical care?"

"I think Dr. Pretelt here is very qualified. He speaks excellent English, and that eases the problem of communication. Hospitals are only 23 miles away in David, and if I really felt I needed the comfort of a U.S. doctor, Miami is just a 2-1/2 hour flight from Panama City."

"What kind of a visa do you have?"

"We don't. Just the tourist card, but we're going to get a *Pensionado* visa this year."

"You're happy here?"

"You bet. I'm doing more and more writing. Jeannie has her painting, and we just bought three horses. They're Colombian Paso Finos. And we hope to start construction on our house in the next 60 days."

"So you're renting?"

"Yes. We have a small 2-bedroom house, furnished, and the water and gardener are included in the rent. $295 per month."

"How about electricity?"

"Power runs about $25, and the phone about $35 – we make a lot of calls to the states. We also have ADSL for our internet connection. Its another $35."

Dan and I decided to have dinner and we moved to the main dining room. The Panamonte really was 'old Panama.' The paneled walls were painted white, large fans whirled slowly overhead, the tables were covered in white linen, and the place settings were silver. Flowers were everywhere. On the tables and in large pots strategically placed around the room.

Dan decided on the fresh *trout almandine*, and I had some beautiful large shrimp with a sweet pepper stuffing. For dessert, I had flan and we both had coffee. With the *jubilato* (senior citizen) discount, the grand total for the two dinners was $20.45. This place has a way of growing on you.

Jim Horton and Marni Craig

Panama is a long way from Peterborough, Ontario, but Jim Horton and Marni made their first trip to the isthmus in 2002. It was a nice break for them. Jim is a Tax Consultant in Canada, and Marni is vice-president of marketing.

The winters in Canada can be darned cold, to say the least, and they wanted a little time in the sun. Jim and Marni spent most of the first December sunning themselves on the Caribbean side of Panama in Bocas del Toro, living on a rented boat. That proved a bit uncomfortable as they had to close all the hatches every night to keep the bugs out. The other problem was: there was more rain in Bocas than sunshine. They had left Canada to enjoy the sun.

To take a break from Bocas, they visited Boquete and really enjoyed their visit. They enjoyed it so much, they bought some property (three building lots) just outside of Boquete.

In the winter of 2004 they returned to Boquete and hired an architect to proceed with their building concept. They knew they wanted a guest cottage, so the plan was to build the small, guesthouse first and live in it while the main house was being built. After moving to the main house, they would then rent the guesthouse.

Under Panamanian Law No. 8, their rental guest-house qualifies as a tourism investment and means they will receive a 20-year exemption on real estate taxes for all assets of their enterprise. That includes the main house.

The guesthouse is small (about 600 square feet) but very functional. Marni had been a commercial caterer and is expert in kitchen design. And, while there is no need for heating or air-conditioning in Boquete, they did include a fireplace. On rainy nights it will be pleasant to have a fire.

Much of the furniture will be teak (Panamanian Teak). They visited one of the custom furniture builders in Boquete and purchased the following items: four bar stools for their kitchen counter; a six-foot dining table with four chairs – two with arms; a queen-size bed; and two chaise lounges for their verandah. All items hand-made from beautiful teak. Their grand total price: $800.

The design of the guest house is special. A local architect drew the plans and they contracted with a Panamanian builder. Floors, of course, are glazed tile, and the ceilings rise to 15-feet which makes the small house seem much larger. There's a lot of glass, and French doors open from the bedroom to the house-length verandah, which is all under roof.

Marni & Friend

I asked Marni about the kitchen. She bought a 4-burner gas range, a washing machine, coffee maker, toaster, 21-inch TV, and a large refrigerator-freezer. Total price: a little less than $1,000. All were new, name-brand items.

Jim talked about their investment. He confided that the building lot, the guesthouse, the main house, and furnishings would total about $100,000. They will probably sell two of the lots over a period of time, and if property continues to appreciate in Boquete, part of their investment will be recouped.

Jim and Marni may speed up their timetable a bit. They were going to finish the guesthouse, come back next winter and build the main house. They may start the main house this spring. That means going back to Canada and probably selling their lakefront home.

I asked them what they liked best about Boquete. Finally, Jim said, "Maybe the question should be, what don't we like about Boquete? The weather is great, prices are good, scenery is spectacular, the Panamanians are lovely people. Maybe they could fix some of the sidewalks. And you have to have a little patience with the bureaucracy – like it took us most of two days to get our tourist cards renewed in David at the immigration office."

Marni smiled. "I'll second all those things. On Wednesdays we sometimes take the bus to David, shop a while, have one of those good pizzas near the *Hotel Gran Nacional*, take in a movie at $1.80 each, and hop the bus back to Boquete. The whole day, including bus trips, pizza and the movie costs us about $10. And, we've had a lot of fun."

Jim chimed in. "And the expatriate social stuff, like the potluck yesterday afternoon at the Santa Lucia Country Club. There were over 80 people there. The food was great, everyone had a good time, and we met some new people as well as renewing some old friendships. One of the neat things is that many of our Panamanian neighbors attend."

I think Jim is right. What's not to like about Boquete?

Kirt Barker

Kirt's father, a professor at Yale, spent several years in Europe as a teaching professor. As a youth, Kirt attended school in Germany and picked up the expatriate life-style at an early age. He has lived in Central America for more than twelve years, and in Panama the last four.

Kirt is an arborist, and is not retired. He received his M.S. degree in Forestry from Yale University, and after his collegiate studies, Kirt did a stint with *Sailing Magazine*.

He has worked in Central America for the World Bank and the U.S. State Department. Obviously, he has a great interest in re-forestation projects and now works closely with the Panamanian government to that end.

Panama, like many countries, was over-logged. Many exotic hardwoods of the tropical forests were ravaged by opportunistic loggers. Teak, coco-bolo rosewood, mahogany, and other rare trees became virtually non-existent. Not only in Central America, but in the tropical forests of the Amazon and Asia. The worldwide thirst for wood was almost inexhaustible.

Choose Panama . . .

When Kirt heard about Panama's re-forestation program he knew this was the place he wanted to be. The country was serious about the preservation of existing forests and the implementation of a new program to continuously replenish and grow new stands of exotic timber.

He immigrated to Panama, bought property and began a new career raising teak and coco-bolo trees. Kirt also has a small *finca* and is in the process of growing vegetables. He's found a new crop in *jalapena* peppers, and is searching for a variety of *habanera* peppers for cultivation.

I found Kirt to be a fascinating young man. He's doing what he wants to do, doing what he believes in, and is doing it in the place he loves most. Panama.

Jim Massey and Leslee Bangs

Jim and Leslee have been married for 28 years. They have two grown sons and three grandchildren. After their family was grown, Jim and Leslee decided to take a break from their jobs. Their home is in the beautiful area of Sisters, Oregon.

Leslee was a committed and experienced city planner, having worked on city staffs and ultimately as a Planning Consultant throughout the west.

Jim is an attorney whose history led him to battling for the underdog. He (and his reputation) came to the attention of country music star, Willie Nelson. Willie was fighting the government bureaucracy and the plight of family farmers facing eviction and the government's seizing of their farms.

Willie convinced Jim to become the leader of his sponsored team of Family Farmers Legal Aid. It became an immensely successful program for America's farmers, and resulted in the saving of many, many families and their small farms. Willie Nelson gave benefit concerts all over America to help fund the legal and courtroom expenses on behalf of our farmers.

Jim is still involved, but not to the extent he once was. Jim and Leslee bought a ketch-rigged Cal 2-46 and sailed the Caribbean. On one of their stops in Panama, they took a trip to Boquete. And, like so many before them, fell in love with the community, and are in the process of building a home here. Because of Leslee's background in community planning, they have also bought some acreage for future development. They've employed a local Panamanian builder and architect for their project.

They still have the sailboat and have no intention of giving up the seafaring life. As Leslee said, "We have the best of all worlds. Cruising the beautiful waters and islands of the Caribbean and having Boquete as our land-based home. We're delighted."

I asked about their children and grandchildren back in the states. "No real problem," Leslee said. "We can get back to the west coast almost as fast as if we lived on the east coast. And, once the home is finished, they can visit us. They'll love Boquete."

Summary

The journey to Panama surprised me.

I found a place where the cost of living was low enough to accommodate a retiree's income.

I found a place where the climate was perfect.

I found a place that offered outstanding medical care and insurance.

I found a people who were friendly, hardworking, and of good humor.

I found a government willing to grant substantial financial incentives to retirees.

I found a place that was within easy travel distance from the States.

I found a place with a safe environment.

I found a place with friendly expatriates from all over the world.

I found cities that were first world.

I found investment opportunities that were outstanding.

I found a place to live.

001

Brief History of Panama

To better understand the *Republica de Panama*, a little history is in order.

Archeologists believe the first inhabitants of Panama arrived between 10,000 and 12,000 years ago. These people were descendents of the migrants who journeyed from Asia across the land bridge of the Bering Sea and migrated southward.

The Spaniards arrived in1501. A Spanish explorer, Rodrigo de Bastidas was the first European to reach the Isthmus. In 1508, Ferdinand V, King of Spain, granted settlement rights to Spanish explorer Diego de Nicuesa. Colonies were established on the Caribbean coast, but the importance of the Isthmus began to be realized when Vasquez Nunez de Balboa led an expedition across the Isthmus to the Pacific coast. He was the first European to see the Pacific Ocean from the Americas, and it became apparent that a relatively short land journey could connect the Atlantic and Pacific oceans.

Shortly after Balboa's expedition, in 1519, Panama City was founded on the Pacific side of the Isthmus. Panama became a market center and crossroads for Spain's conquest of the Americas. Gold and silver (plundered from the Incas) were transported from Peru to Panama City, then carried across the Isthmus to waiting ships in the Caribbean harbor of Portobelo.

These riches made both Panama City and Portobelo targets for pirates. The pirates of the Caribbean, epitomized by Henry Morgan and Sir Francis Drake, preyed on cities and caravel's alike. Panama City, Cartagena, and Portobelo were targets for plunder as well as centers for the slave trade.

The Viceroy of Peru governed Panama until 1718 when The Viceroy of New Granada was created by Spain. This territory included present-day Colombia, Ecuador, Venezuela and the Isthmus.

In the mid-1800's, Spain's empire in South America began to crumble. The fever of independence swept through the colonies. In 1821, Panama declared its independence from Spain and decided to become part of the new Republic of Colombia.

For eighty-two years, Panama was treated like a stepchild. Panamanians began making their own laws, and grew distant from Colombia. They also grew apart culturally from the rest of Colombia, becoming less religious, politically more liberal, and more open to the outside influence of Britain and the United States.

Britain and the United States realized the importance of Panama lay in its narrow land mass, and began to compete for the rights to control the transit of goods and people from the Atlantic to the Pacific. The sea route around Cape Horn was long and treacherous. The possibility of a canal was born, and the preferred route was either Nicaragua or the Isthmus.

Choose Panama . . .

American businessmen took the lead when they financed and constructed a railroad across the Isthmus, completed in 1855. After the discovery of gold in California, transportation of goods and people flourished, and for a while the Panama Railroad was the most profitable in the world. Businesses to serve travelers boomed on both sides of the Isthmus.

In the late 1870's, French diplomat Ferdinand de Lesseps, who had built the Suez canal in Egypt, called a conference in Paris to implement a sea level design and raise money to build a canal across Panama. Work started in 1882, but the project was beset by many problems. Tropical disease, equipment delays, financial problems, and poor planning forced the project into bankruptcy.

In 1902, Teddy Roosevelt and the Congress authorized buying and rehabilitating the French route. The United States negotiated a treaty with Colombia for construction rights, but the Colombian senate refused to ratify it. Rebellions by locals in Panama against Colombian rule and violence occurred frequently. The increase in the number of U.S. citizens and businesses in the area fanned the flames.

The U.S. sent its Marines to Panama to preserve law and order, to protect the lives and property of American citizens and businesses, and to repel Colombia's military efforts to prevent Panama's independence. While still a province of Colombia,

Panama was on its way to becoming a U.S. protectorate. It declared its independence on November 3, 1903.

Within two weeks, a treaty was signed giving the U.S. construction rights to build the canal. The terms of the treaty gave the U.S. a perpetual lease for a section ten miles wide, stretching from the Atlantic to the Pacific. Within this zone, the U.S. could exercise complete control, including the canal's operation and military occupation. The canal was completed in 1914.

Panama had limited resources. For years, its biggest asset was the income derived from the lease, but roads, hospitals, utilities, and schools were still built by Panama. The Republic was dependent on the canal-zone for water, jobs, imports, transportation, and military security.

Resentment of U.S. domination began to grow. Relations with the U.S. deteriorated in the 1950's, and remained strained for thirty years.

In 1977, President Jimmy Carter negotiated a new treaty with Panama that provided the canal be turned over to the Republic on December 31, 1999. The treaty allowed the U.S. to maintain a military presence, but more of the canal income would accrue to Panama during the years between 1977 and 2000. On the turn-over date, the U.S. relinquished all rights to the canal and withdrew its military.

In 1983, Manuel Noriega, former head of Panama's intelligence service, became head of the National Guard and assumed power. Noriega did not hold political office, but as commander of the military and the police, he controlled the government. Noriega used the military to imprison, torture, and murder opponents and those who disagreed with his policies. At one time, Noriega had been an informant of the CIA, but drifted into major affiliations with the drug cartels. In the late 1980's, the U.S. withdrew its support of the government.

In 1988, Noriega was indicted by a U.S. court on drug charges. He fomented riots and street demonstrations against the U.S., removed a duly elected President of Panama and nullified the election results. Tensions rose between Noriega's armed forces and the U.S. military. The U.S. invaded Panama on December 20, 1989 with the stated goals of arresting Noriega to face drug charges, restoring democracy, and protecting American lives and business interests.

The invasion was controversial. It violated international law, yet it was welcomed by the majority of Panama's citizenry as the only way to rid itself of Noriega and his brutal, corrupt regime. He is now in prison, and if he ever gets out, he is wanted by the French Government.

In 1994, Perez Balladares was elected President. He instituted wide economic reform, reduced the size of government, and initiated programs to attract foreign investment. The Panama Canal Authority was formed to take over the duties of managing the canal in 2000. The U.S. and the Panamanian government cooperated fully to make the transition smooth and trouble-free.

Panama assumed control of the canal, military bases, and adjacent facilities on December 31, 1999. For the first time since the 16th century, Panama had assumed control of all of its territory, and relations with the U.S. blossomed. The resentment of America being a political and military occupier of their country has dissolved into one of welcome and friendship.

Frequently Asked Questions

Q. Can we bring our pets to Panama?

A. Yes. Check with a Panamanian attorney who will help with forms etc. Cost will be about $140. per animal.

Q. What's the best way to ship our household goods?

A. Containers – 20 or 40 foot, depending on the amount of goods. The cost will be $3,000 to $4,000 – not including packing. The best advice is to sell most everything before you leave.

Q. Do I have to pay duty on household goods?

A. Not if the goods are "used."

Q. Should I bring a car?

A. Shipping a car can be difficult. Duties are about 8% unless you've obtained a *Pensionado Visa*. Some people include their car in the same container as their household goods.

There's a lot of red tape, forms, and bureauocracy in shipping a car. Ask your forwarder about 'roll on, roll off' for a car.

Q. Is it necessary to get shots?

A. No. Shots are not required to visit Panama. However, there is no 'downside' to get the big three: Typhoid, Hepatitis, and Tetanus. Yellow fever is not a problem unless you travel to uninhabited parts of the jungle.

Q. Are credit cards readily accepted?

A. Visa, MasterCard and American Express are generally accepted everywhere. Travelers Checks are something of a problem. Your bank ATM or debit card is a necessity.

Q. Do I need a Visa to visit?

A. No. Your only requirements are a passport and Tourist Card.. The Tourist card ($5) is available from the airline or upon arrival in Panama.

Q. How about currency exchange?

A. The only paper currency in use is the U.S. dollar. The Panamanian currency is officially the 'Balboa' but it has been pegged at the U.S. dollar since 1903.

Q. Climate?

A. Panama is tropical. The year round daytime temperature in the coastal areas will average 80-90F. In the highlands, 70-75F, but at night, you'll need a sweater.

Q. Can foreigners own property?

A. Yes. They have the same rights as citizens.

Q. Do I have to speak Spanish?

A. The literacy rate in Panama is 97%. English is a required subject in schools. It is estimated 25% of the population now speak English. However, buy a Spanish Lesson CD before you visit, and take lessons after you arrive.

Panama Embassies and Consulates

If Panama requires you to have a visa for visiting, they can be obtained from an Embassy or Consulate. This does not apply to visas for residency, such as the *Pensionado Visa*. Residency visas can only be obtained in Panama.

At the time of this writing, the only countries which Panama requires a passport <u>and</u> a visa were Chad, Ecuador, Egypt, the Philippines, Peru, the Dominican Republic, and Thailand.

Visitors from the following countries need a passport <u>and</u> a tourist card: Antigua, Australia, Bahamas, Belize, Bermuda, Bolivia, Brazil, Canada, Chile, China, Colombia, Denmark, Granada, Greece, Guyana, Iceland, Ireland, Jamaica, Japan, Malta, Mexico, Monaco, the Netherlands, New Zealand, South Korea, Taiwan, Tobago, Trinidad, The USA, and Venezuela.

Visitors from the following countries need only a passport: Argentina, Austria, Belgium, Costa Rica, El Salvador, England, Finland, France, Germany, Guatemala, Honduras, Hungary, Israel, Italy, Luxembourg, Paraguay, Poland, Northern Ireland, Scotland, Singapore, Switzerland, Uruguay, and Wales.

Choose Panama . . .

If the name of your country does not appear, call the
Panamanian Embassy or Consulate nearest you or
(507) 227-1448.

Panamanian embassies are maintained in the following
countries: Brazil, Canada, Colombia, Costa Rica, El
Salvador, France, Germany, Guatemala, Honduras,
Israel, Italy, Japan, Mexico, Nicaragua, Singapore,
Spain, UK, and the USA. Australian citizens should
contact the Panamanian embassy in Singapore.

Some countries have Panamanian consulates. In the
US, there are consulate offices in Chicago, Honolulu,
Houston, Los Angeles (Anaheim, CA), Miami, New
York, New Orleans, Philadelphia, San Diego, and San
Francisco. The embassy is in Washington, DC.

Helpful Web Sites

www.panamainfo.com

www.panamadera.com

www.internationalliving.com

www.escapeartists.com

www.vistamarresort.com

www.altosdelmaria.com

www.escapetoboquete.com

Choose Panama . . .

Index

Choose Panama . . .

About the Author

Bill Hutchings started his writing career as a technical writer, freelancing for NEC, Texas Instruments, Business Automation, National Microware, Venture Software, and others.

After several years of writing about data base management applications, he wrote his first travel book, *Radio on the Road ...the Traveler's Companion.* This book enjoyed six editions and thirteen printings.

Bill spent three months in Mexico doing research for a novel, *The Gold of Guadalupe,* before making his trip to Panama. He fell in love with the people and life on the Isthmus. A second novel, *The Counterfeit Affair,* is scheduled for completion in the fall of 2004.

Printed in the United States
52133LVS00001B/94-99